The Beading on Fabric Book

INTERSTELLAR

TRADING & PUBLISHING COMPANY

LA MESA, CALIFORNIA

ISBN 0-9645957-8-8
LIBRARY OF CONGRESS CATALOG NUMBER: 97-93598
SAN: 298-5829

Copyright © 1999 Wendy Simpson Conner
Published 1999 by The Interstellar Publishing Company
All rights reserved. No part of this book may be reproduced in
any manner (mechanical, electronic, or photographic);
nor may it be transmitted or stored in any retrieval
system; nor copied for public or private use
(other than "fair use ") without the written
permission of the author.

Illustrations by Wendy Simpson Conner
Color Photography by Don Brandos
Printed in the United States of America

Visit our website at www.interstellarpublishing.com

FIRST PRINTING: APRIL, 1999

ACKNOWLEDGMENTS:
To Jennie, Priscilla, Joni, and Paul;
and everyone who bought and loved
THE BEST LITTLE BEADING BOOK,
THE BEADED LAMPSHADE BOOK,
THE MAGICAL BEADED MEDICINE BAG BOOK.
THE 'KNOTTY' MACRAME AND BEADING BOOK
THE BEADED WATCHBAND BOOK
THE CHAIN & CRYSTAL BOOK
THE BEADED JEWELRY FOR A WEDDING BOOK
THE CHILDREN'S BEADING BOOK
THE CAT LOVER'S BEADED PROJECT BOOK
THE WIRE BENDING BOOK

Introduction

I remember sitting on the porch in the sun when I was very young, sewing beads onto a scrap of fabric. I did such a beautiful job, I couldn't wait to show my mom. Unfortunately, when I stood up, I realized that I had sewn my beautiful creation to my skirt. I just KNEW when I showed this to her, mom would allow me to cut the skirt to save the beaded piece. Alas, this was not the case, and I cried as we cut the threads off the skirt. Nowadays, I try to be more careful when I'm beading!

Many of my childhood memories involve the embellishing of fabrics with beads and buttons. My mother sews beautifully, and made most of our clothes and costumes. Those "recreational" shopping trips to the fabric stores are forever ingrained in my memory. I loved to play in my grandmother's huge tins of old buttons. My father was from England, and told us of the Pearly Men. They were men who covered their suits in buttons that they found (usually pearly, hence their name).

There is a joy that comes when you create a fabric of beads. There is something so satisfying about handling this beaded art; it has a weight and a balance, and when you are done, you feel a little wonderment that you are the one who made this gorgeous design with substance. Beaded fabric goes back thousands of years; if you visit The Bead Museum in Arizona, you will see wonderful examples. There are as many varieties as there are cultures.

The projects in this book have global influences; the picture frame (on the cover) is inspired by the Kuba beaded collars in Africa; the beaded bodice pieces are from my grandmother's work that she did for the Ziegfeld Follies; the rosette is a very basic Native American design; the beaded purses were popular in the 20's.

I hope you enjoy this book. This is part of a series of 25 books called **The Beading Books Series.** Other books in the series include The Best Little Beading Book, The Beaded Lampshade Book, The Magical Beaded Medicine Bag Book, The "Knotty" Macrame and Beading Book, The Beaded Watchband Book, The Chain & Crystal Book, The Beaded Jewelry for a Wedding Book, The Children's Beading Book, The Cat Lover's Beaded Project Book, and The Wirebending Book.

As always, I love hearing your wonderful comments. Please feel free to write to me c/o The Interstellar Trading and Publishing Company, Post Office Box 2215, La Mesa, CA 91943. You can also email me at Interstlr@aol.com, or visit our website at www.interstellarpublishing.com

Happy Beading!™   "Me"

The Beading on Fabric Book

Table of Contents

Fabrics..5
Threads..7
Stitches..8
Supplies..11
Color Photos Index..12
Full Color Photos..13-16
Beads and Sequins..17
Seedbeads...18
Beading a Sweater..19
Making a Beaded Box...20
Bracelets on Leather...22
Sectional Belt..24
Leather Pouch with Rosette..25
Beaded Fabric Tassel #1...27
Beaded Fabric Tassel #2...30
Beaded Fabric Tassel #3...32
Beading on Netting...33
Beaded Dress Bodices...34
Beaded Purse #1...38
Beaded Purse #2...41
Beaded Medallion...45
Kuba-inspired Picture Frame..47
About the Author..51
Other Books Available..52

Fabrics

You can bead just about any fabric you desire. Some keep their shape, and you'll have no trouble working with them. Others are more difficult, and tend to stretch or crease. There's no definite rules; it's best to experiment with small swatches before you begin a project to see if you like the way the fabric looks, and how it drapes with beads on it.

Cotton Fabrics

This would include canvas, denim, duck, muslin and similiar fabrics (like linen). 100% natural fibers tend to wrinkle, so you may want to work with a blend (combined with synthetics) if you're beading a jacket or dress. These look wonderful when beaded, and if you do a solid bead design on them, they are substantial enough to support the beads, and allow for their weight.

One of the newest innovations is a treated linen that is supposed to be wrinkle-free. This also works up nicely.

Aida Cloth

Also known as "counted cross stitch cloth". This has a larger, open weave and comes in different sizes. #22 works with smaller beads (like size 13/0 seedbeads) and #14 (size 11/0 seedbeads) It gives you structure in an intricate beading design, and you can adapt needlepoint and any graphed pattern to make any number of objects.

Satin

This is a little trickier to work with, as it creases easily. Satin is usually a rayon-blend, and you must be careful when you iron it . . . use a presscloth, and always iron on the wrong side. Iron before you bead, olthertwise you will get the imprint of the beads in your fabric. Also, if your needle is not sharp enough, it will pull and run the fabric as you stitch. Always use the finest size needle with the sharpest point possible, and stitch carefully. Don't use a needle that you've used on a coarser fabric, as this will dull your needle and damage your satin.

The Beading on Fabric Book

Leathers and Suedes

Working on stiff leather is a bit of a challenge, because you want a needle fine enough to pass through your beads, yet strong enough to penetrate the leather. "Sharps" needles, if they're fine enough to go through the bead, are the best. English beading needles also work with softer leather.

Soft leather is a delight to bead, as is machine washable suede, a synthetic that is very easy to care for.

Netting

This is one of the best fabrics for beading appliques. It has strength and transparency, and can be laid right on top of another fabric and be virtually invisible.

Knits

Knits are definitely the trickiest to bead. We love them because they "give", yet it's the stretch that causes the problems when we bead. If you stitch too tightly, when the knits pull, the threads will snap and break. The best way to deal with this is to use a fusable interfacing on light weight knits. This will restrict the range of stretchiness, but you will have a more substantial base for your beadwork. It is recommended that you don't apply really heavy beads, as knits tend to warp and lose their shape.

Silk and Wool

There are so many variations out there, that the best thing to do is to make a small sampler with your intended fabric before you begin. Some silks are so delicate, that if you look at them sideways, they stain and wrinkle. Others are heartier, and will be more practical in the real world. Wools come in many varieties also, and some can be quite expensive. Again, you can save a lot of time and money with the sample piece first.

Knitted Garments

Seedbeads can get lost in the larger weaves. If using smaller beads, work with a smaller weave. Large beads work well on bulkier pieces.

Threads

The best threads will remain intact for years to come. The worst ones have no longevity, and all your hard work goes for nothing. One very basic consideration (and this applies to fabric, threads, and beads) is the method you use to keep your beaded garment clean. Your fabric may be wash-and-wear, but your thread is not. A hot dryer will make your beadwork pucker, because some threads shrink. Another consideration is the dry cleaners. The wrong chemistry can dissolve your thread (and your beads)! Test your combination (thread, fabric and beads) in a small sampler before you begin something massive. You may even want to test your cleaning method on your sampler, and switch to a heartier combination if necessary.

Nymo
This is a very sturdy nylon thread that comes in different sizes. From thinnest to thickest, they range from 00, 0, B, D, F, and G. Usually available in black or white, you may be fortunate enough to locate it in colors to match your fabric (green, red, blue, and my personal favorite, beige - it goes with everything).

Cotton
Many of my grandmother's beautiful pieces that she did for the Ziegfeld Follies were worked on cotton thread. Where there once was a beautifully stitched piece, now remains a handful of beads and the rotted short pieces of cotton thread. Cotton will not last; the hard work you put into your piece will not guarantee an heirloom if you use cotton. Opt for something longer lasting.

Dental floss
Yuk! I always picture dental floss being used for its intended purpose. This is really not recommended for beading, as it is about as biodegradable as you can get. it stretches and shrinks, and in the end, it breaks. Use it on your teeth, and invest in Nymo instead.

Monofiliment
Both you and your dry cleaner will end up in tears if you use this one. It is so incredibly heat reactive, a very hot day will do it in. Don't use it. Again, you're better off with Nymo.

The Beading on Fabric Book

Stitches

The variety of stitches is almost endless, and you may find certain ones that you use for sewing work well for you in beading on fabric. These are just a few easy, popular stitches that work up quickly.

The Back Stitch

A good stitch that anchors beads securely.

The Running Stitch

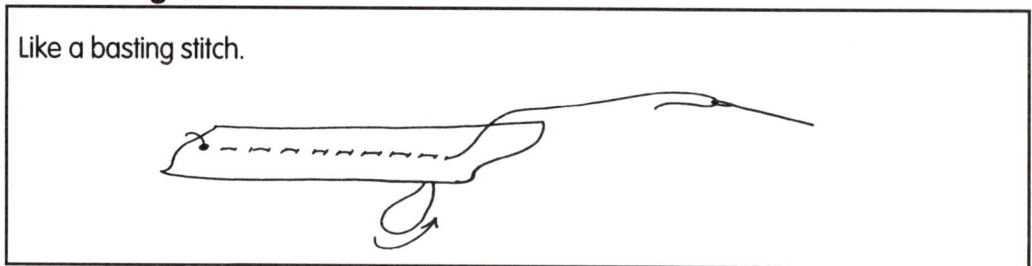

Like a basting stitch.

The Continental Stitch

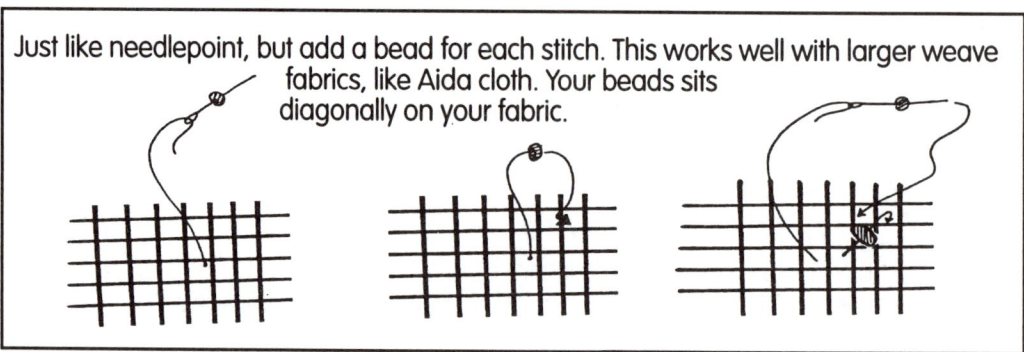

Just like needlepoint, but add a bead for each stitch. This works well with larger weave fabrics, like Aida cloth. Your beads sits diagonally on your fabric.

The Beading on Fabric Book

The Staystitch

Also known as the "tacking stitch"

This will lock your knot into place, so it can't pull out.

Stitching Sequins

One method is to use a bead to hold the sequin in place.

Another method (this works for machine stitching, also) is to sew thru the hole of the sequin, and overlap them to cover the holes.

The Satin Stitch

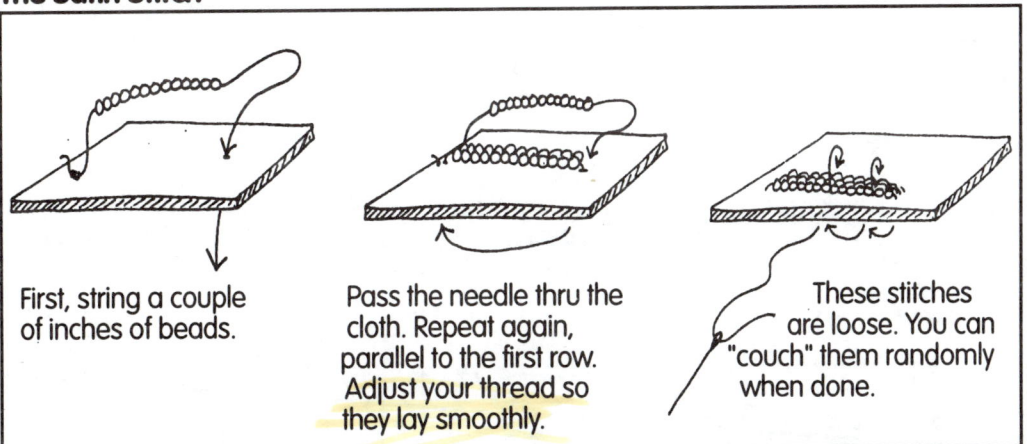

First, string a couple of inches of beads.

Pass the needle thru the cloth. Repeat again, parallel to the first row. Adjust your thread so they lay smoothly.

These stitches are loose. You can "couch" them randomly when done.

Three Bead Method

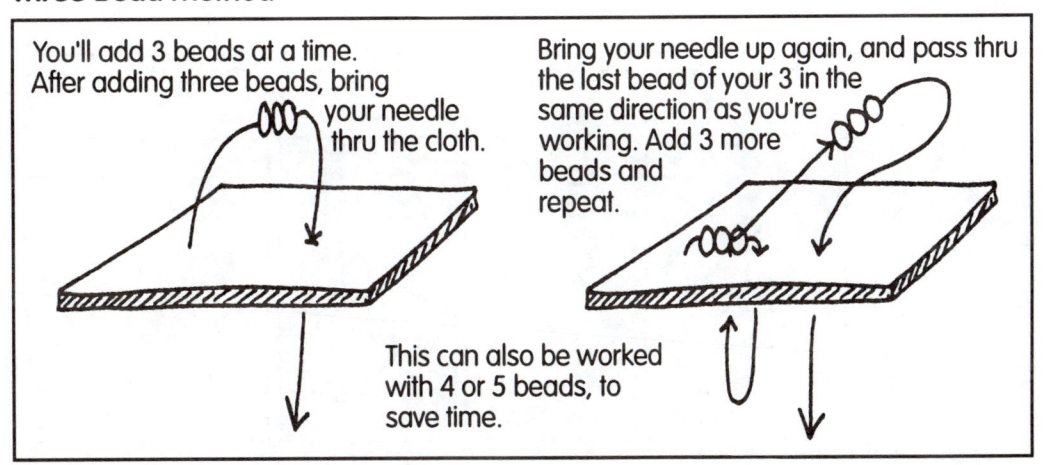

You'll add 3 beads at a time. After adding three beads, bring your needle thru the cloth.

Bring your needle up again, and pass thru the last bead of your 3 in the same direction as you're working. Add 3 more beads and repeat.

This can also be worked with 4 or 5 beads, to save time.

The Beading on Fabric Book

Couching - One Needle Method

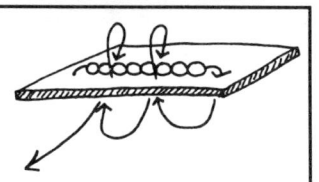

After you stitch, circle back and tack down your stitches.

Couching - Two Needle Method

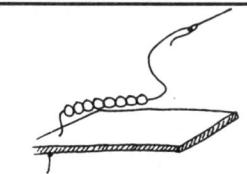

The first needle strings the beads onto one long strand. The second one catches the first thread to tack it down randomly. Many dresses are beaded this way, because intricate designs can be achieved. Unfortunately, it's not very strong, or practical for solid bead coverage.

Edging Stitches (Use for borders and to finish fabric edges)

Picot Edging

Makes a nice, finished edge. Can also be worked with any odd number of beads (1,3,5, etc.)

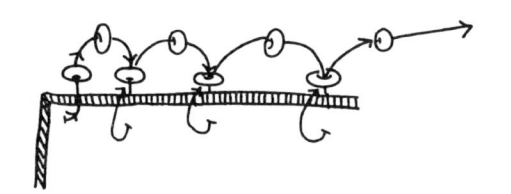

Whip Stitch

Work in a circular motion, letting your thread wrap over the edge as you work.

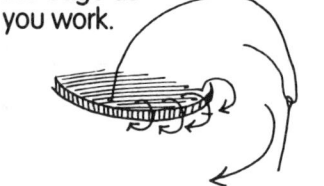

Fringes

Fringes are a fun way to end your edges.

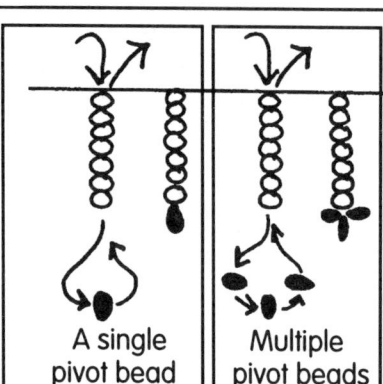

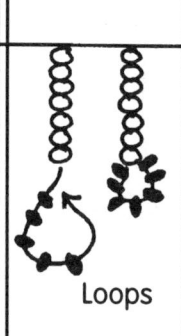

- A single pivot bead
- Multiple pivot beads
- Loops
- Using a charm or crystal

The Beading on Fabric Book

Supplies

It doesn't take much to bead on fabric, but having the right stuff sure does help.

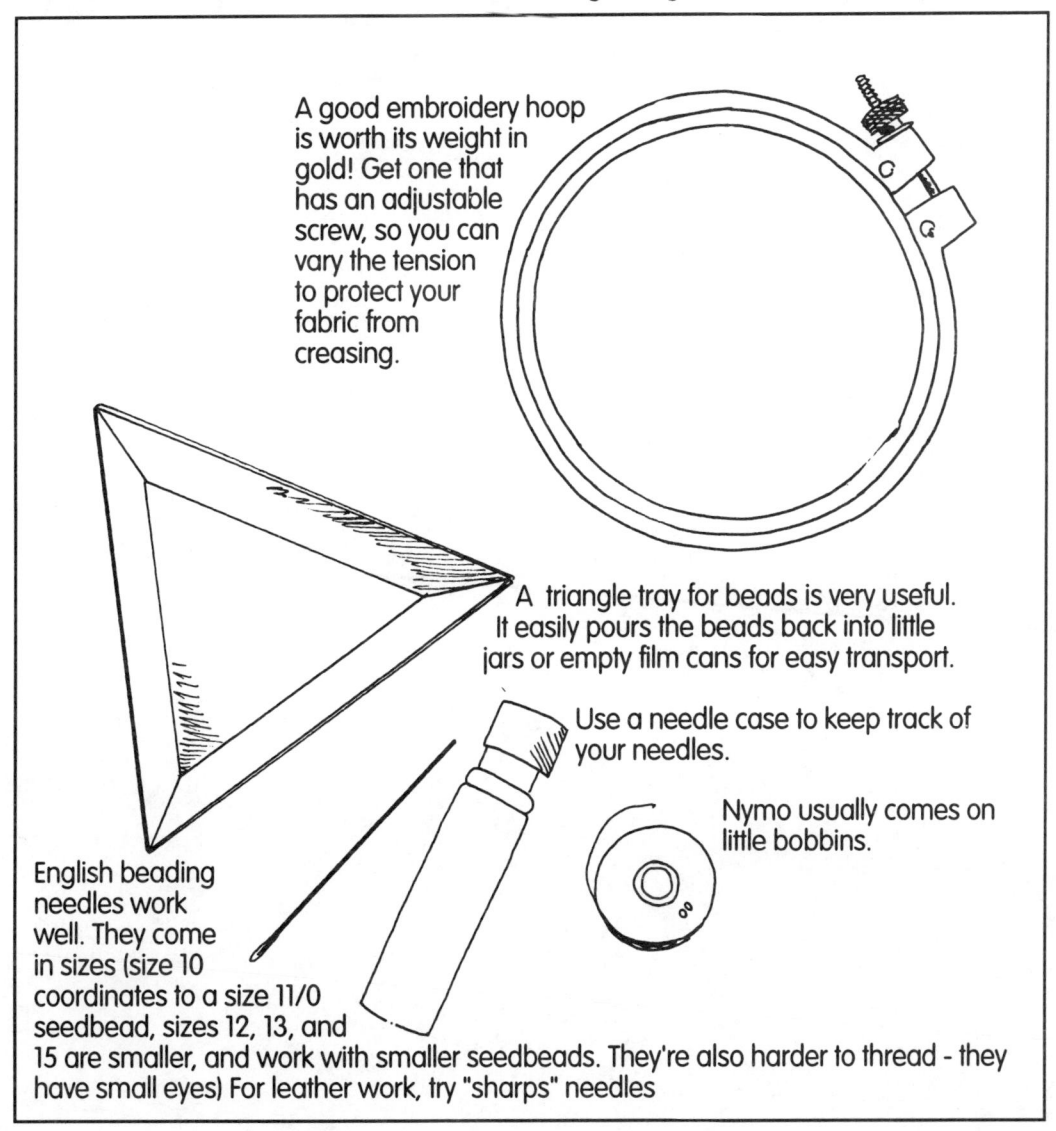

A good embroidery hoop is worth its weight in gold! Get one that has an adjustable screw, so you can vary the tension to protect your fabric from creasing.

A triangle tray for beads is very useful. It easily pours the beads back into little jars or empty film cans for easy transport.

Use a needle case to keep track of your needles.

Nymo usually comes on little bobbins.

English beading needles work well. They come in sizes (size 10 coordinates to a size 11/0 seedbead, sizes 12, 13, and 15 are smaller, and work with smaller seedbeads. They're also harder to thread - they have small eyes) For leather work, try "sharps" needles

The Beading on Fabric Book

Color Photo Index

Kuba-Inspired Picture Frame..Front Cover

Beaded Satin Purses..Page 13

Three Beaded Bodice Appliques,
Beaded Sectional Belt..Page 14

Beaded Fabric Tassels,
Applique Lace Dress Piece,
Three Appliques,
Beaded Cabochon with Fringe...Page 15

Rosette on Leather Pouch,
Beaded Box, Bracelets,
Embellished Sweater...Page 16

Beaded Medallion..Back Cover

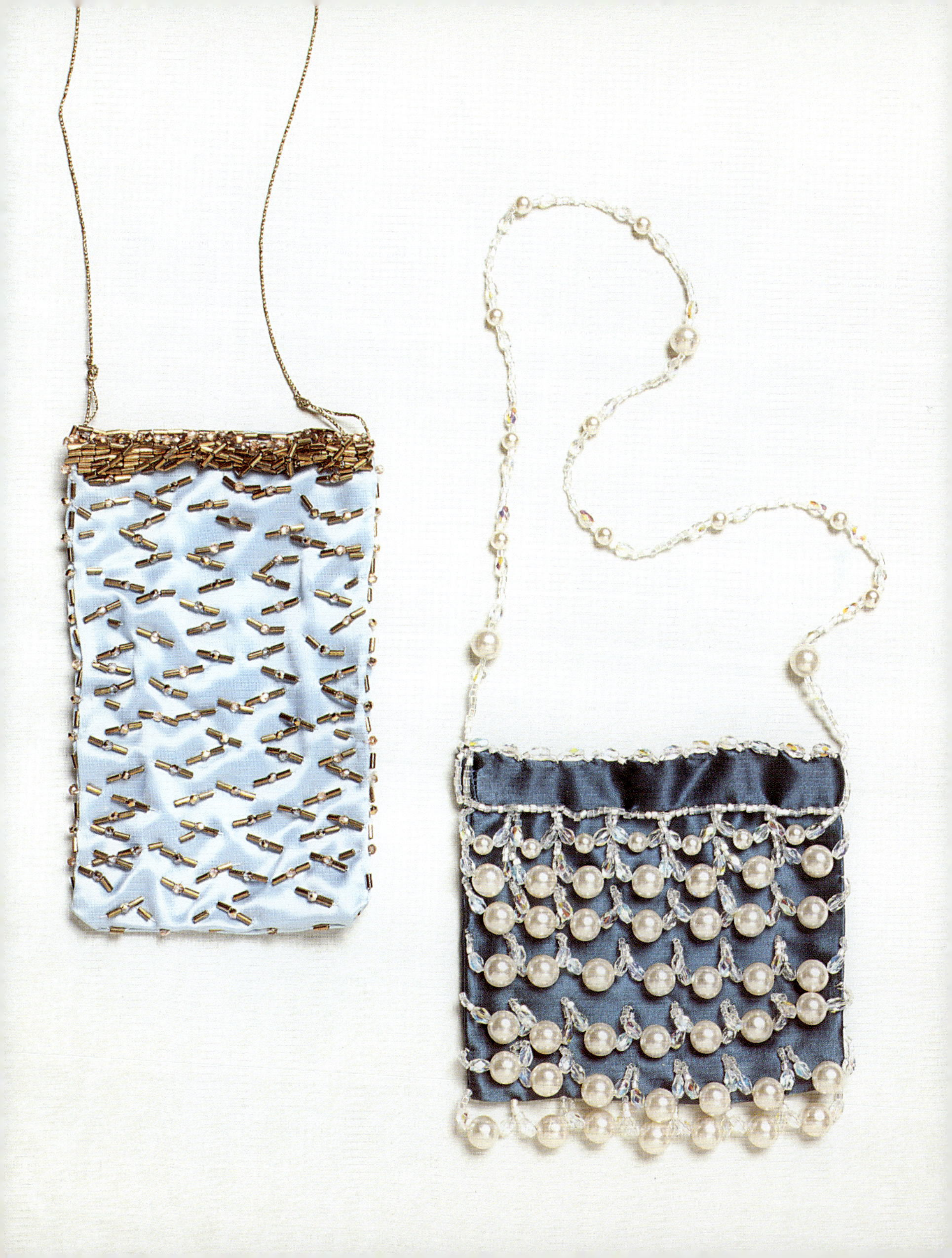

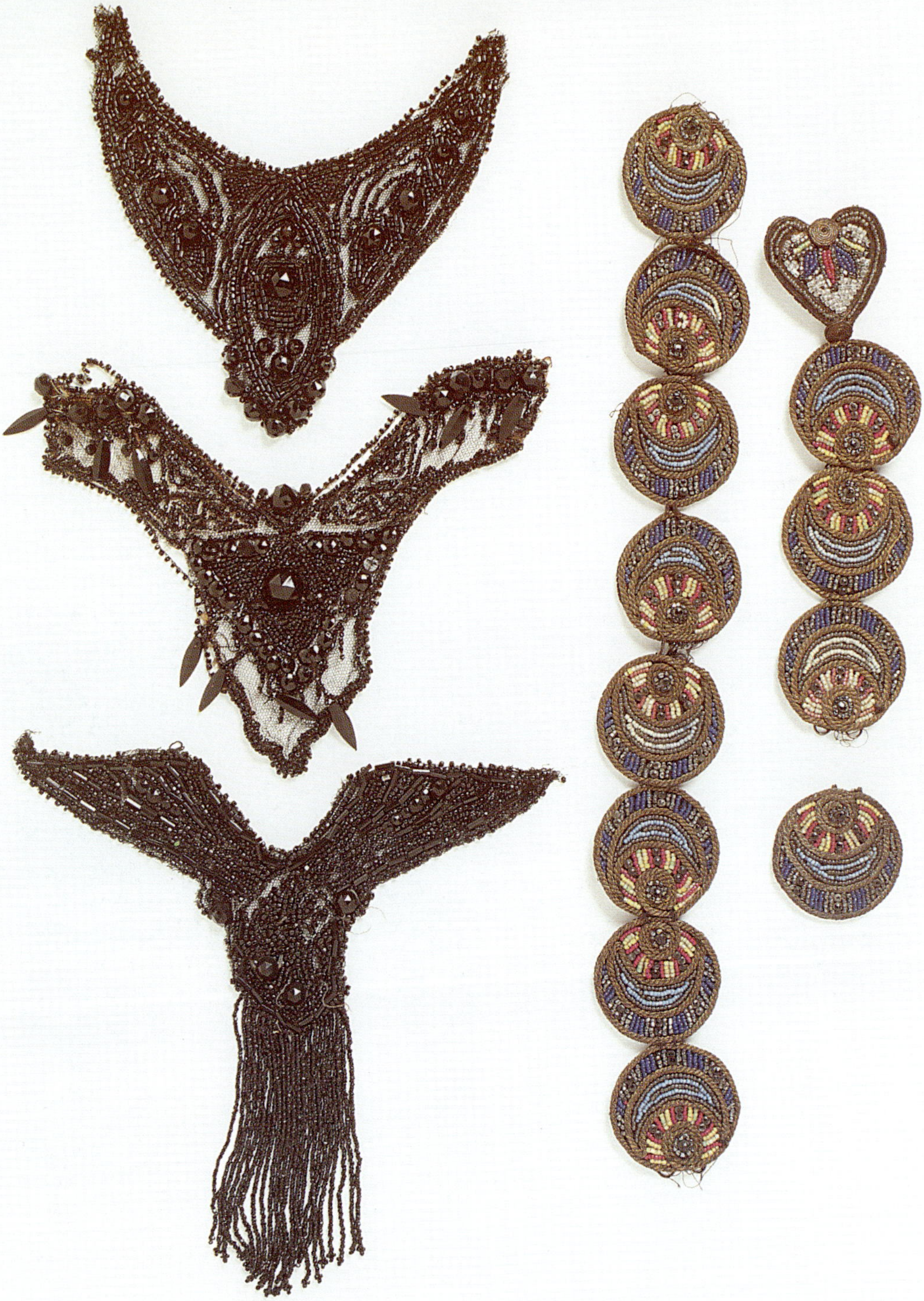

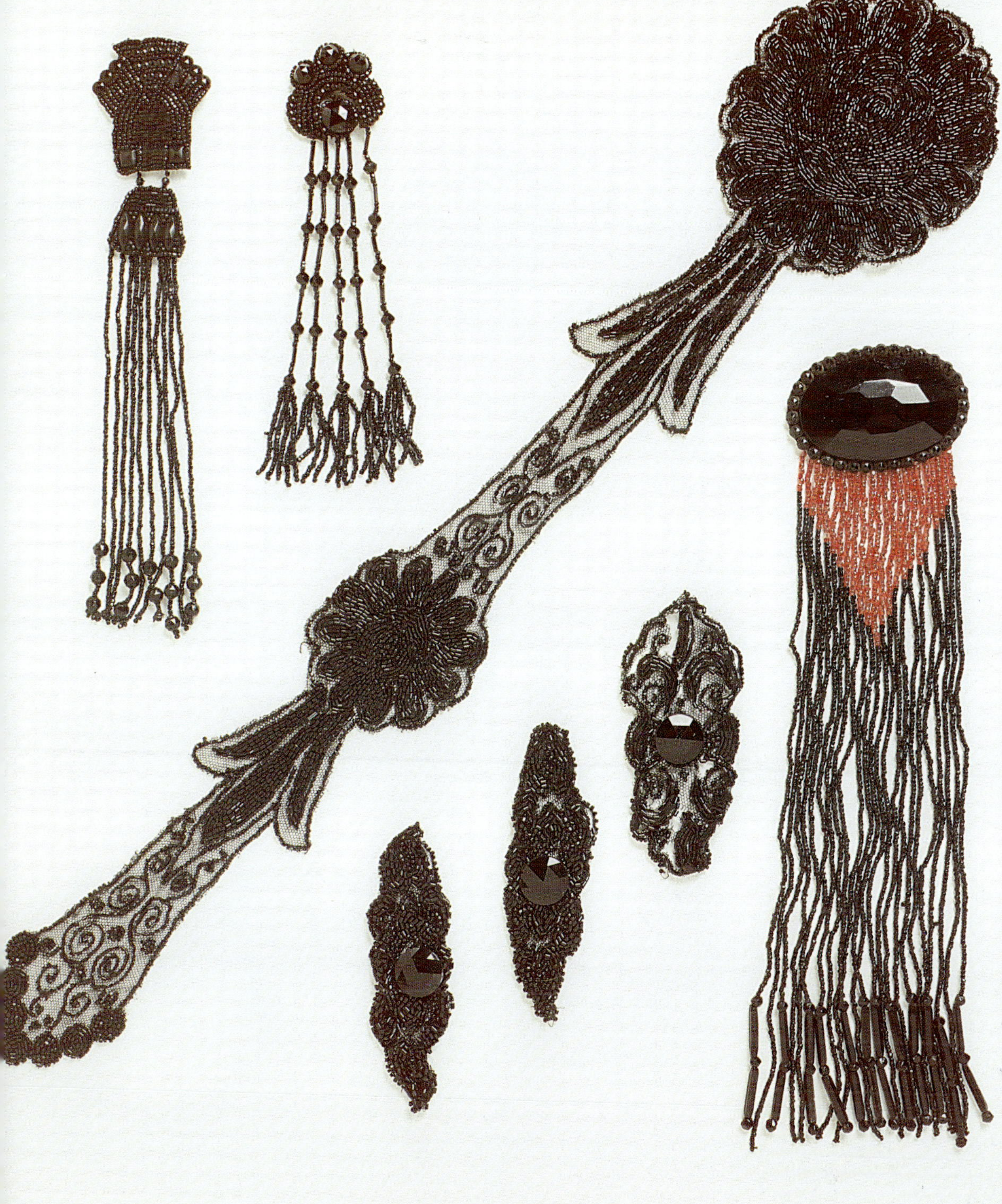

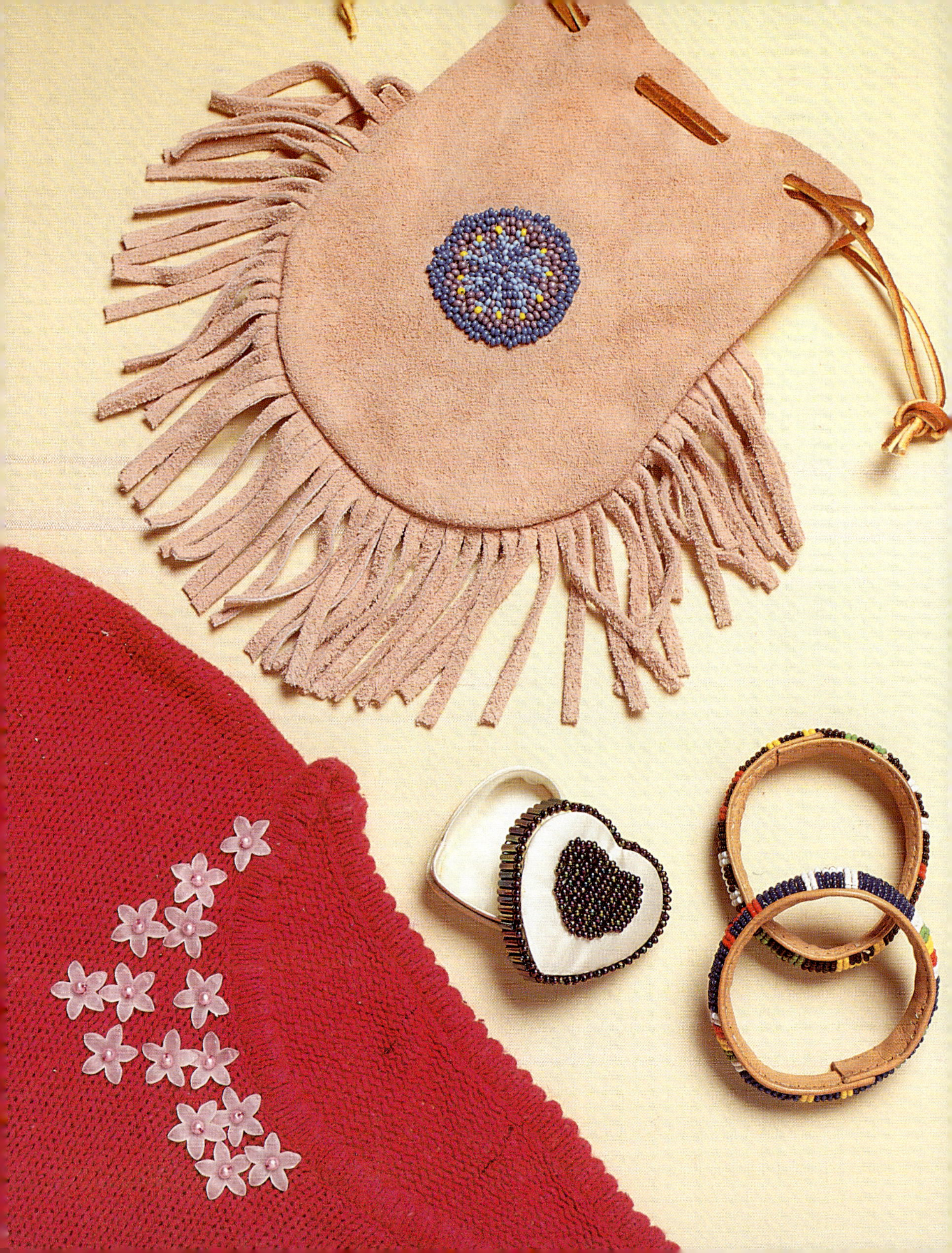

Beads and Sequins

There is no end to what can be beaded to fabric. Your choices are endless, and a particular piece can look very different depending on the materials you work with.

Seedbeads
By far the most useful, you see these on just about everything beaded. They're small, and fill in the gaps. There are many varieties. Be sure that the ones you choose are colorfast, so they don't bleach out when drycleaned or exposed to light. The chart on the following page shows you the range of sizes available.

Buglebeads
Like seedbeads, these are also used quite often for beadwork. You would use the English beading needles with these and seedbeads. Again, colorfastness is an issue.

Sequins
Great for filling in large areas, they are very inexpensive and give a definite "look" to your beaded piece.

Cabochons
These flat-backed, undrilled stones are beautiful when you bead around them. Because they are undrilled, they're not stitched to the fabric, but cemented or glued. Be sure to use a strong cement that will bond it to the fabric and withstand any cleaning or washing if it is on a garment. There are specially-made fabric adhesives that do this.

Cowrie Shells
Used a lot in African beadwork, they are very beautiful when teamed with seedbeads.

Pearls
Real freshwater pearls can't withstand drycleaning. Glass or plastic are a good alternative, but show your pearls to your drycleaner before you bead the garment. Many cleaning processes will dissolve the less expensive plastic pearls

Miscellaneous
Try buttons, jewelry findings, seeds, wooden beads, etc. If you're making an ornamental piece that you won't be drycleaning, then your options are endless.

The Beading on Fabric Book

Seed Beads

Seedbeads are measured by a very unusual method. They're not sized like other beads; rather, by the size of the rods used for making the glass beads (measured in increments called "aughts", which are roughly equivalent to 1/2 centimeter. Aught means "0"). The smaller the number, the larger the bead. Thus, 11/0 is smaller than 7/0.

Seedbeads also have different finishes. Some are colorfast, and some are not. Always test a bead before you work it into an extensive project.

Some of the styles of seedbead that are used for beading fabric include:

CEYLON - Also called "pearl", has a glossy, creamy ("pearlized") finish.
CHARLOTTE BEAD - Traditionally used in Native American beadwork, a size 13/0 opaque seed bead that is cut and faceted like crystal.
"E" BEAD - A size 6/0 bead.
FROST - Frosted finish
HEXAGON-CUT - Bead cut with 6 sides; reflects light.
INDIAN BEAD - An opaque "pony" bead.
IRIS - Translucent, glossy appearance.
LUSTRE - Has a very glassy, "bright" quality
OPAQUE LUSTRE - Glossy, deep color
THREE-CUT - Highly reflective bead, with three surfaces showing at one time. This really catches the light.
TILE CUT - A very squared cyllindrical bead that weaves well due to its uniformity (like a short bugle bead. Works great for peyote or other weaving stitches.
TRANSLUCENT - "French Opal"
TRANSPARENT - clear glass
TWO-CUT - Reflective bead, with two surfaces showing at one time.

Size
16/0
15/0
14/0
13/0
12/0
11/0
10/0
9/0
8/0
7/0
6/0
5/0
4/0
3/0
2/0
1/0

Beading a Sweater

Beading a neckline is a great way to dress up a plain sweater or sweatshirt.

MATERIALS:

- Plastic pearls
- Plastic flowers with center hole (available in craft stores)
- Nymo or a good nylon sewing thread that is colorfast. It's nice if your thread matches the sweater.

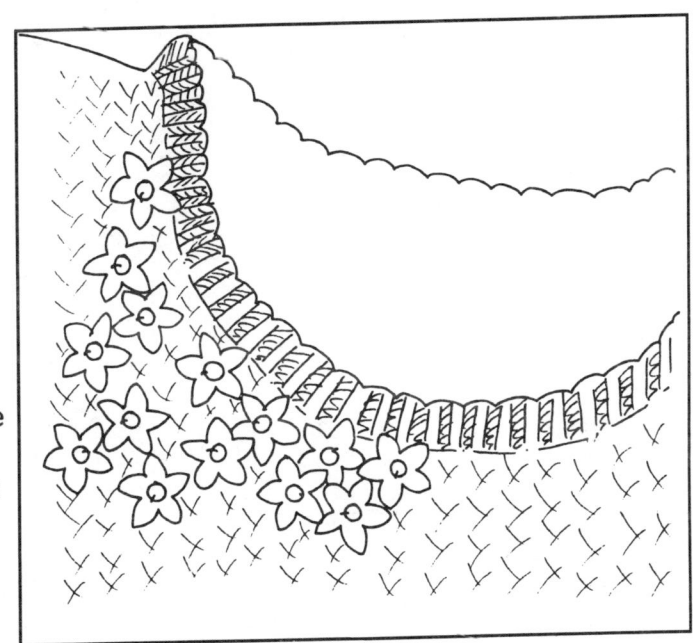

Layout your flowers and decide where you want them. Make a knot in the ends of your thread, and work with a double thread. Secure the knot with a couple of staystitches, as knots tend to pass through the loose weave of sweaters.

Add your flower, then your bead. Pass back thru the hole in the flower, and secure to the sweater. Do this for each of your flowers.

The Beading on Fabric Book

Beaded Box

Simple little fabric boxes are available just about everywhere. These can be dressed up with beads.

MATERIALS:
- Fabric box
- Size 11/0 Seedbeads *
- Bugle beads *
- #10 English beading needle
- Nymo thread

*Depending on the box, one hank should be plenty)

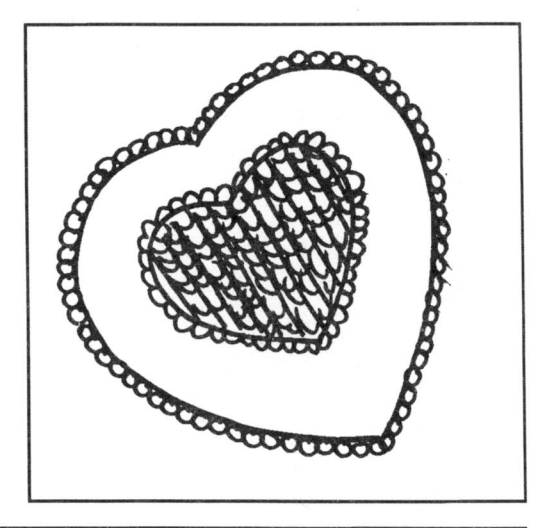

Bead the side of the box lid first. Work single thread, securing your knot. This will be hidden as you work your beads. Add your bugle beads to the side of the box.

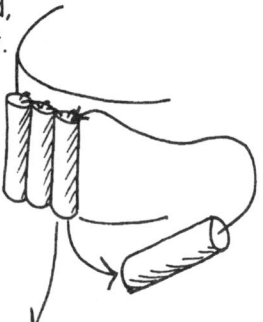

Anchor your beads to each other, then secure by sewing them to the box. Work completely around the box lid edge.

Cap the bugle beads with seedbeads to give a nice edge.

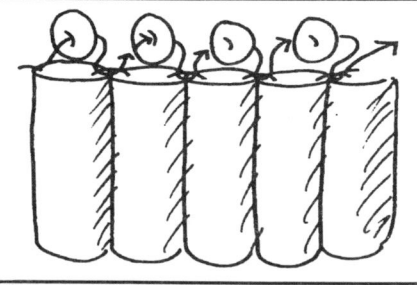

The Beading on Fabric Book

Draw a design on the top of the box. Using the Three Bead Method (see page 9) outline your design in seedbeads.

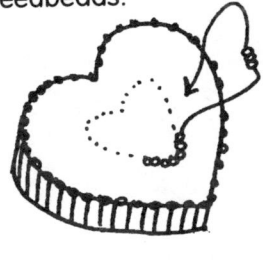

Fill in the pattern with the Satin Stitch.

Another alternative is to make a box out of Aida cloth. This can be beaded over an existing cardboard box, or you can make your own pattern.

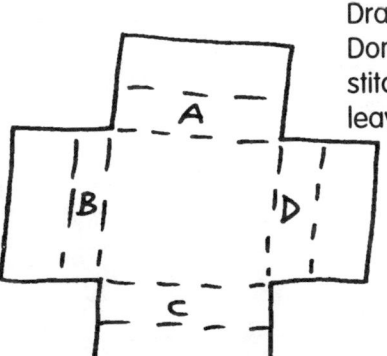

Draw out your design, and use an embroidery hoop. Don't cut it out until you are done. Use whatever stitches or design you like. Don't forget to leave a seam allowance.

Fold your flaps underneath the sides of the box. Form it over cardboard for strength.

Make a bottom for your box. Don't bead it; cover it with a coordinating fabric.

The Beading on Fabric Book

Bracelets on Leather

This bangle bracelet is a real attention-getter. Influenced by the beaded bracelets from Africa, they are easy to make and fun to wear.

MATERIALS:
- Piece of leather, 3" x 12"
- A variety of 11/0 seedbeads
- Sharps beading needle (small enough to pass thru beads)
- A scrap piece of fabric, 2"x12"
- "B" weight nymo thread
- One sewing machine
- White glue

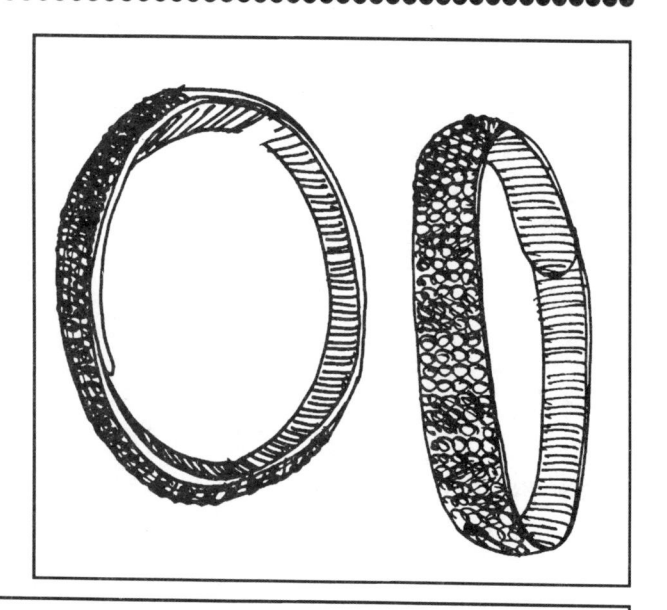

Fold your scrap fabric in half lengthwise. Fold again, so it is about 1/2" wide. Machine sew on the long open edge then press.

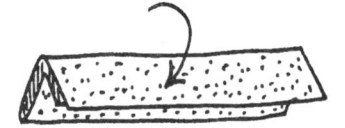

Lay the fabric on the wrong side of the leather. Use glue to secure. When dry, fold edges of leather over as shown.

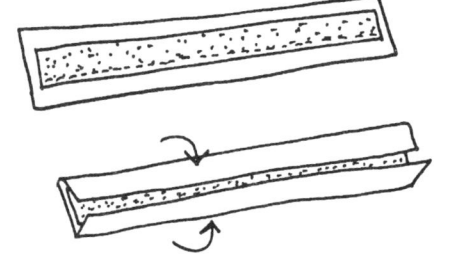

The Beading on Fabric Book

Handsew the leather edges over the fabric with the backstitch. You now have a cushioned length of padded leather. If your sewing machine can handle the thickness, sew along both top and bottom edges to create a ridge.

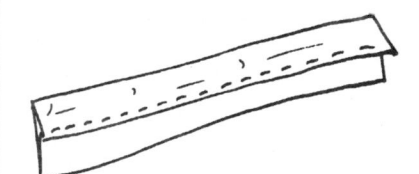

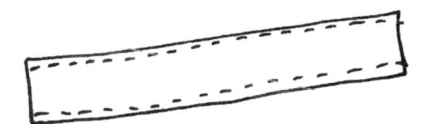

Measure your wrist. Cut the length of leather the size of your wrist + 3" (this will depend on how loose or tight you like your bangle bracelets. Adjust for personal taste. Overlap the edges by 1/2", and sew into a bracelet with the seam side out. Make sure you have stitched this securely, as this is the structure for your bracelet. You don't want this coming apart!

Using the satin stitch, bead the outside of the bracelet. Leave a "lip" about 1/8" from both top and bottom edges, and sew into your line of stitches. Don't go all the way thru the leather, the stitches will show on the other side. Stitch right over the seam that joined your bracelet together. Finish your ends with several stitches.

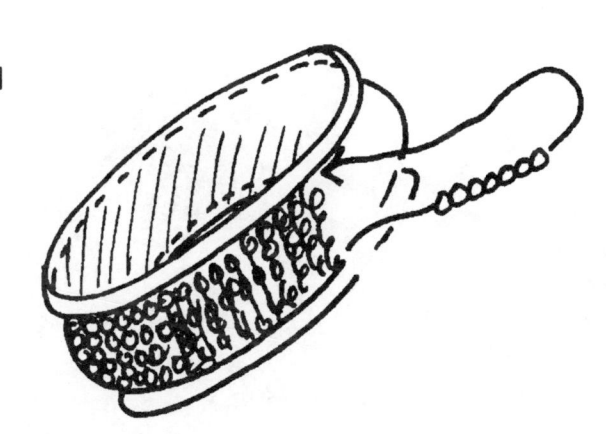

The Beading on Fabric Book

Sectional Belt

This is one of my grandmother's designs for the Ziegfeld Follies. The Sectional Belt was popular among the performers, because it could be worn by anyone, no matter what size. The secret of the belt is that its made up of modular beaded medallions, each a mirror image. They're attached by hook-and-eyes, and depending on the size of the wearer, one could add or subtract components for an appropriate fit.

You can purchase circles of leather already cut and bead on those, or use a circular leather cutter (or circular matte cutter, available in arts and craft stores to cut your medallions.

Decide on a design, and repeat it. You can scan your design on a computer, then flop the image, so you have mirror images in your design.

MATERIALS:
- Circles of leather approximately 2" in diameter.
- A variety of seedbeads
- Sharps beading needle (small enough to pass thru beads) and #10 English beading needle
- Hooks and eyes
- Nymo

*A HANDYHINT:
Beading on leather is not always easy when you want to use smaller seedbeads. You can work your medallions on canvas, duck, or Aida cloth, cut them to the size of your leather backing, and glue in place. If you whip stitch over the edges, no one will be the wiser.

The Beading on Fabric Book

Leather Pouch with Rosette

This Rosette can be beaded right onto the leather, or onto Aida cloth and then stitched (as an applique) onto the bag. This is the method I recommend - you won't damage your bag, and you can center your design when you attach it.

MATERIALS:
- One leather pouch
- Seedbeads
- Sharps beading needle small enough to pass thru beads and #10 English beading needle
- Aida cloth and embroidery hoop (optional)
- Nymo

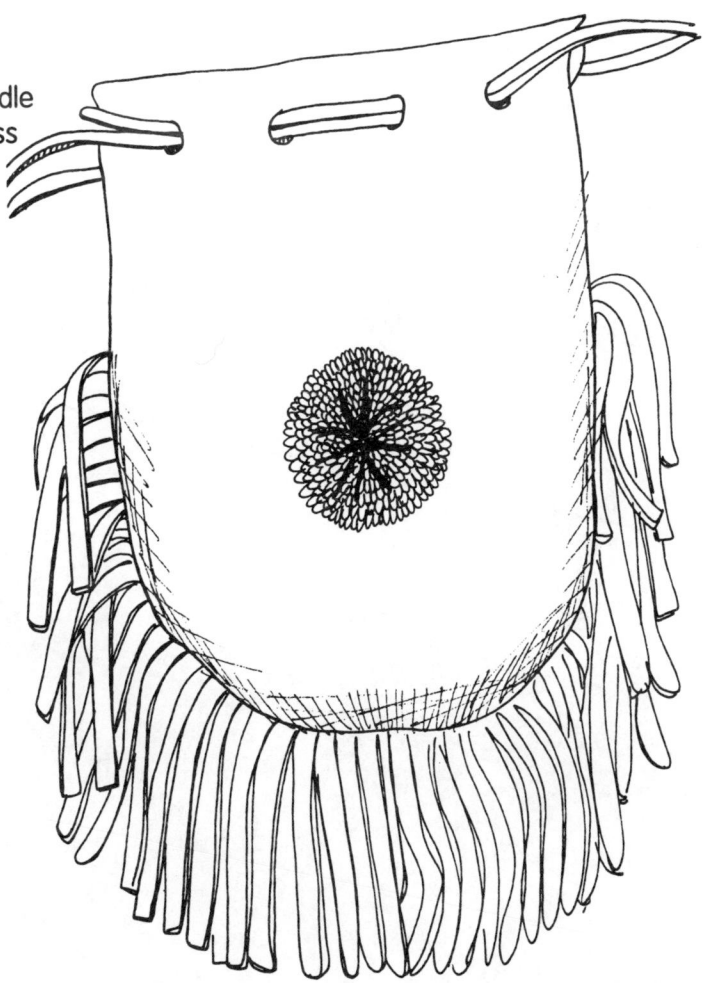

The Beading on Fabric Book

STITCHING A ROSETTE:

If you would like to make a pattern, it's best to draw it first so you have a design to work from.

Lay out your main beads in 4 rows. The holes need to be facing sideways, not the center. Work outward, tacking each bead in line.

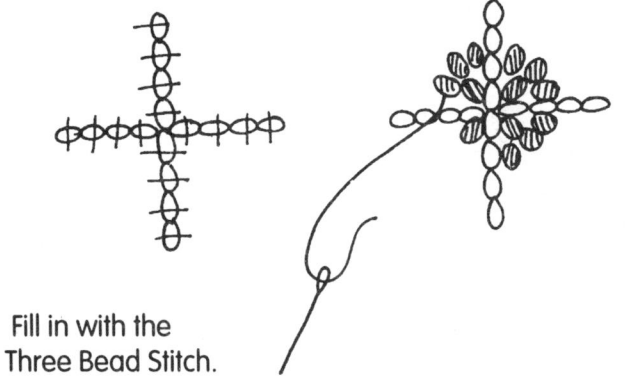

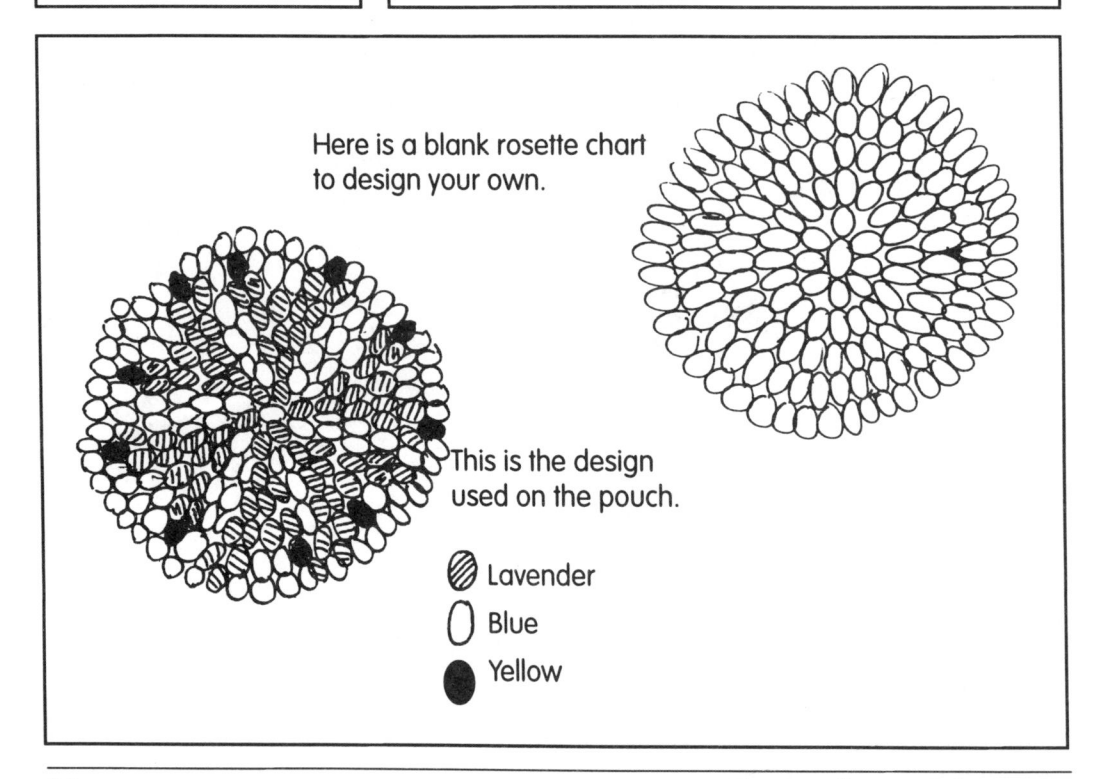

Fill in with the Three Bead Stitch.

Here is a blank rosette chart to design your own.

This is the design used on the pouch.

- ⦸ Lavender
- ⦾ Blue
- ⬤ Yellow

The Beading on Fabric Book

Beaded Fabric Tassel #1

Beaded Fabric Fringes were very popular as ornamentation for dresses and coats in the early part of the century. This is one from my grandmother's collection.

MATERIALS:
- Stiff black fabric for backing
- Black 3-cut seedbeads
- #10 English beading needle
- Embroidery hoop (optional)
- "B" weight black nymo
- Twentyfive black 6mm round faceted crystal
- Black faceted cabochon, 14mm wide
- Three black faceted cabochons, 8mm wide
- twentyfive black bugle beads
- Jeweler's cement

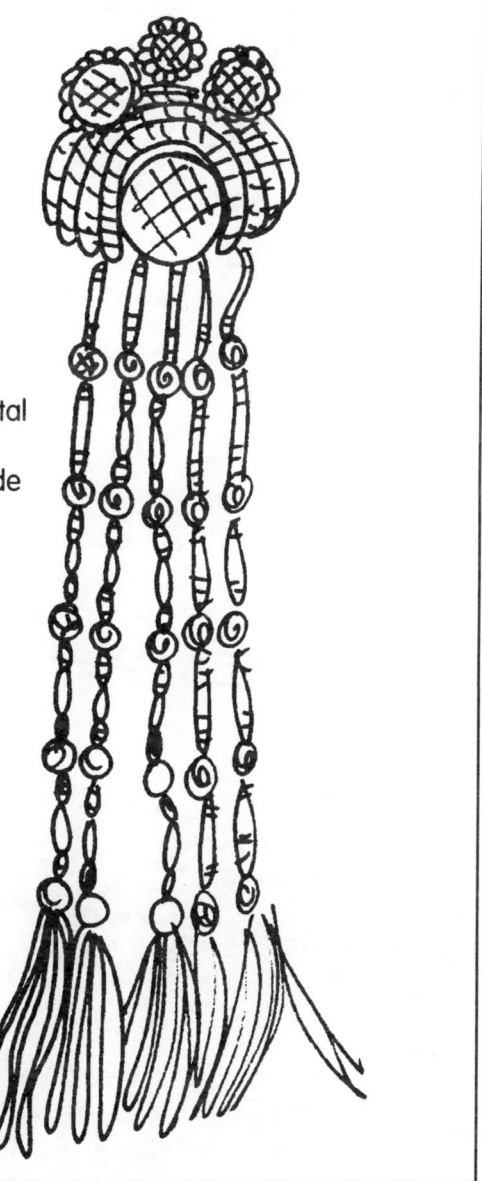

The Beading on Fabric Book

Draw your design on your fabric.

Vintage looks work best with this. Cut out your design. If your fabric frays easily, seal the ends with jeweler's cement. The backing for the 14mm cabochon is a separate piece of fabric.

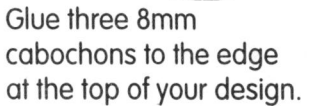

Glue three 8mm cabochons to the edge at the top of your design.

Using the 3 Bead Method, bead an outline on the with your three-cut black beads. Use the Whip Stitch to finish your edges.

Fill in your pattern in the flow of the piece.

Add your 14mm cabochon, and bead around the edge.

The Beading on Fabric Book

Add your fringes, using a mixture of crystals, seedbeads and bugle beads as shown.

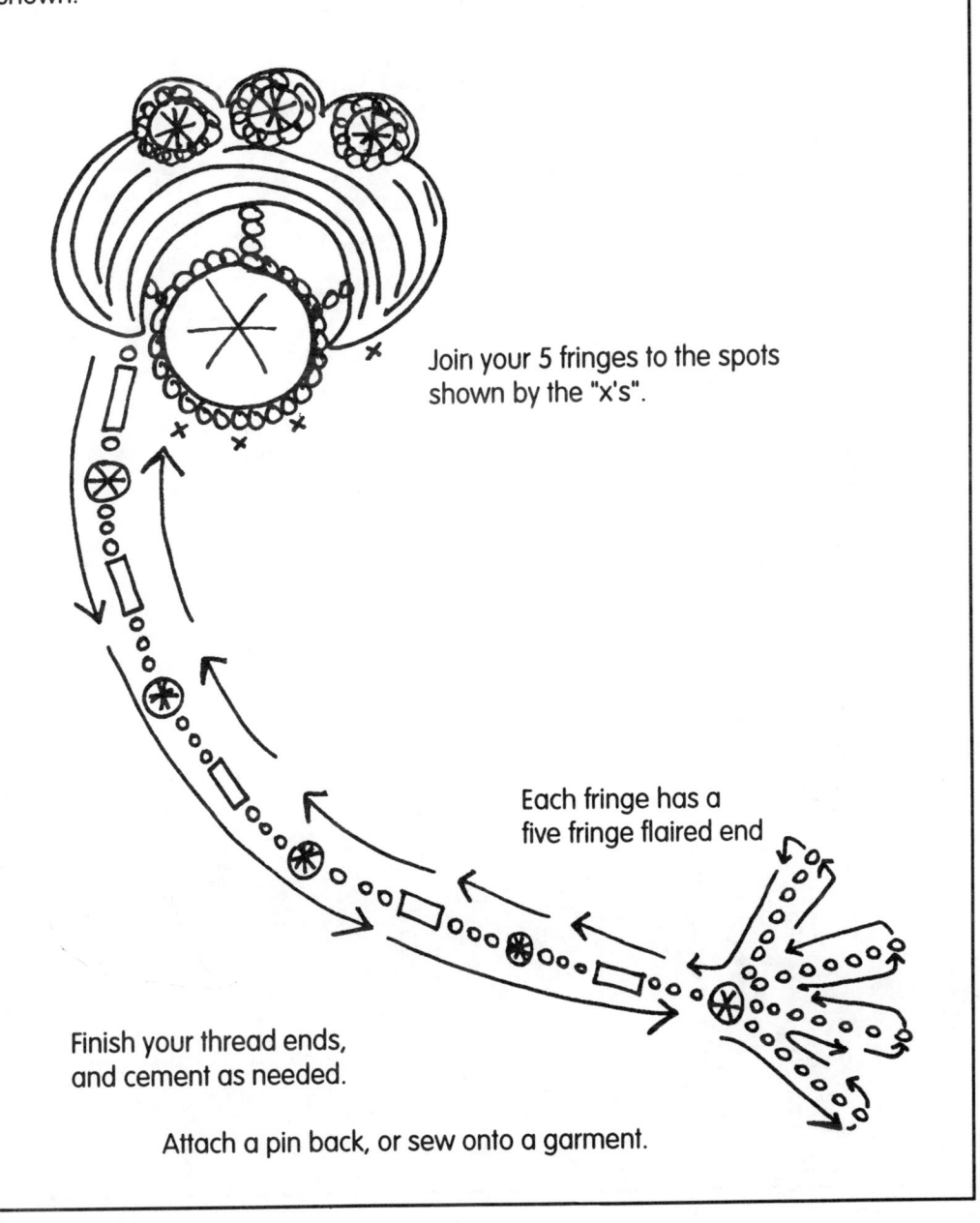

Join your 5 fringes to the spots shown by the "x's".

Each fringe has a five fringe flaired end

Finish your thread ends, and cement as needed.

Attach a pin back, or sew onto a garment.

The Beading on Fabric Book

Beaded Tassel #2

This is also from my grandmother's collection. This tassel is more ornate than the first. It has two tiers, but the fringe is simpler.

MATERIALS:
- Stiff piece of black fabric
- Black 3-cut seedbeads
- #10 English beading needle
- Nymo thread (0 or B weight)
- Fifteen black 6mm faceted crystal
- A variety of black faceted cabochons,
    - Six 5mm round
    - Two 6mm square
    - Five Marquis shape
- Jeweler's cement

Draw your design onto your fabric.

Add your cabochons

Fill in with your beads.

Join the top and bottom parts of your design, and add your fringe.

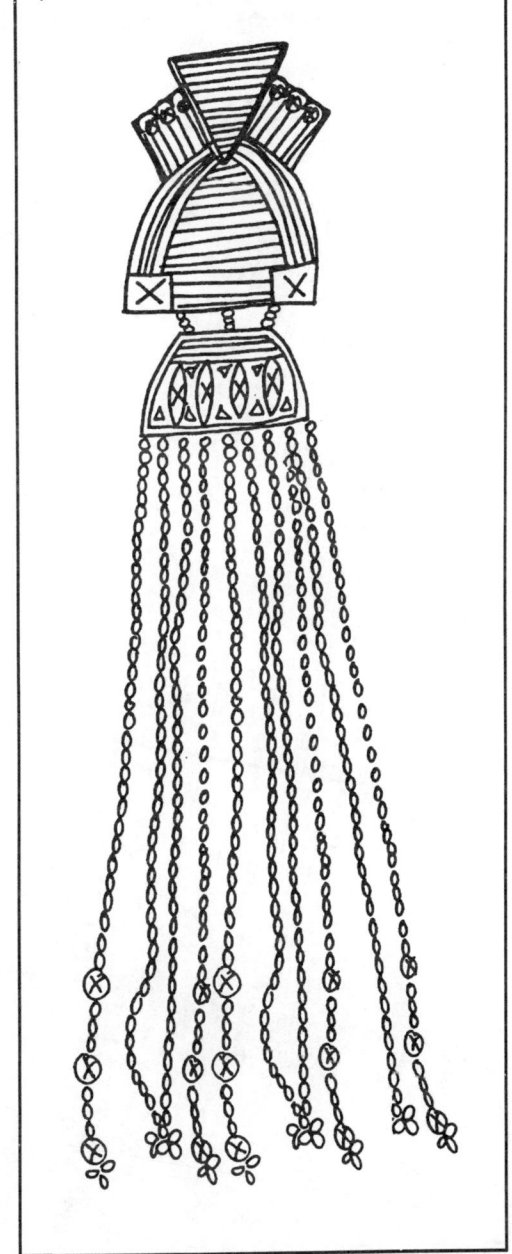

The Beading on Fabric Book

Beaded Tassel #3

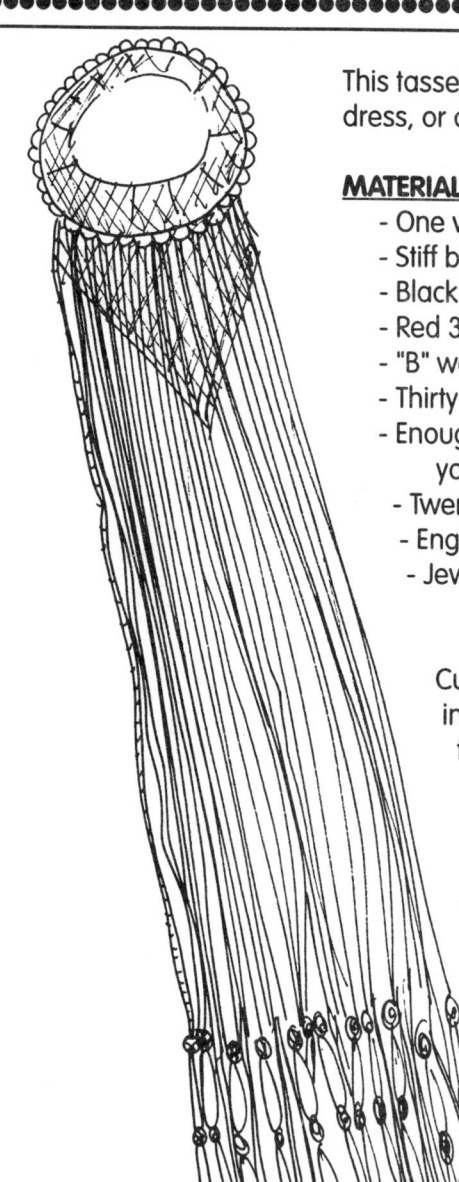

This tassel is stunning on the front of an evening dress, or as a very dramatic necklace.

MATERIALS
- One very large faceted cabochon
- Stiff black fabric or black leather
- Black 3-cut seedbeads
- Red 3-cut seedbeads
- "B" weight nymo thread
- Thirty-six 5mm black faceted crystal beads
- Enough 5mm black crystal beads to circle your cabochon
- Twenty-four black long bugle beads
- English beading needle size #10
- Jeweler's cement

Cut your fabric to fit your cabochon. Cement into place, but leave an area at the bottom that is not cemented fully. This is so that you can hide your stitches under the cabochon.

Using the Three Bead Method, bead around the cabochon with the 5mm black crystal. Whip Stitch the edges for a more polished look.

Work your fringe as shown, with a "V" in red seedbeads.

Finish your ends, and cement the rest of the cabochon to the backing. Add a pin back, attach to a dress, or make into a necklace.

The Beading on Fabric Book

Beading on Netting

Many appliques are worked on netting. An applique is an adornment that is worked on a separate piece of fabric, then added to the garment after it is done.

Netting is wonderful to work with; it is virtually invisible when added to a garment, yet strong enough to hold the weight of the beads.

Many vintage pieces were worked in this way. There is a delicate quality, yet strength too.

It is popular for those times when high-quantity production is required. It is very portable and easy to handle.

You can work large areas of netting on stretcher bars or large embroidery hoops; you can also work with smaller hoops for greater control.

I've seen beads of all types worked on netting, but for the best look, I suggest not using beads that are too large. They do tend to distort and pull the shape.

Seedbeads seem to look the best; you can cover the netting in a dense, intricate pattern. Mix this with crystal, buttons, cabochons, etc.

The Beading on Fabric Book

Beaded Dress Bodices

Taking the beadng on netting one step further, you can create beautiful beaded dress bodices that look like something from Titanic. These appliques were very popular, because if a dress wore out, or became unwearable, the intricate beadwork of the applique could be saved and put onto another dress.

Embellish with beads, cabochons and crystals. You can make them as ornate as you like.

The beaded dress bodices shown are all from my grandmother's collection.

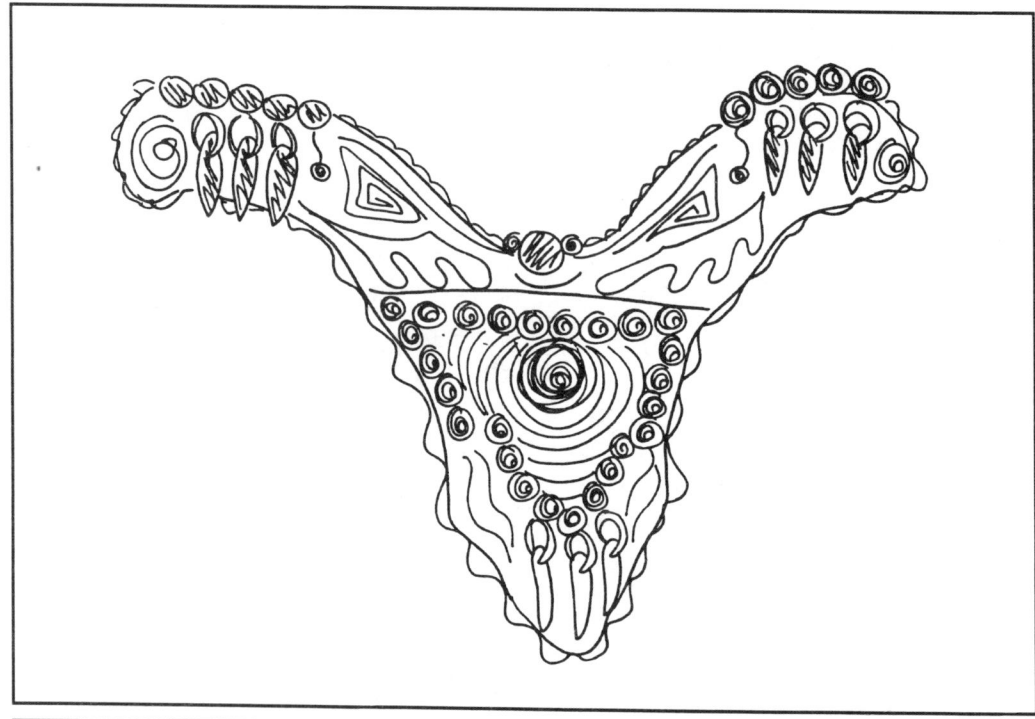

The Beading on Fabric Book

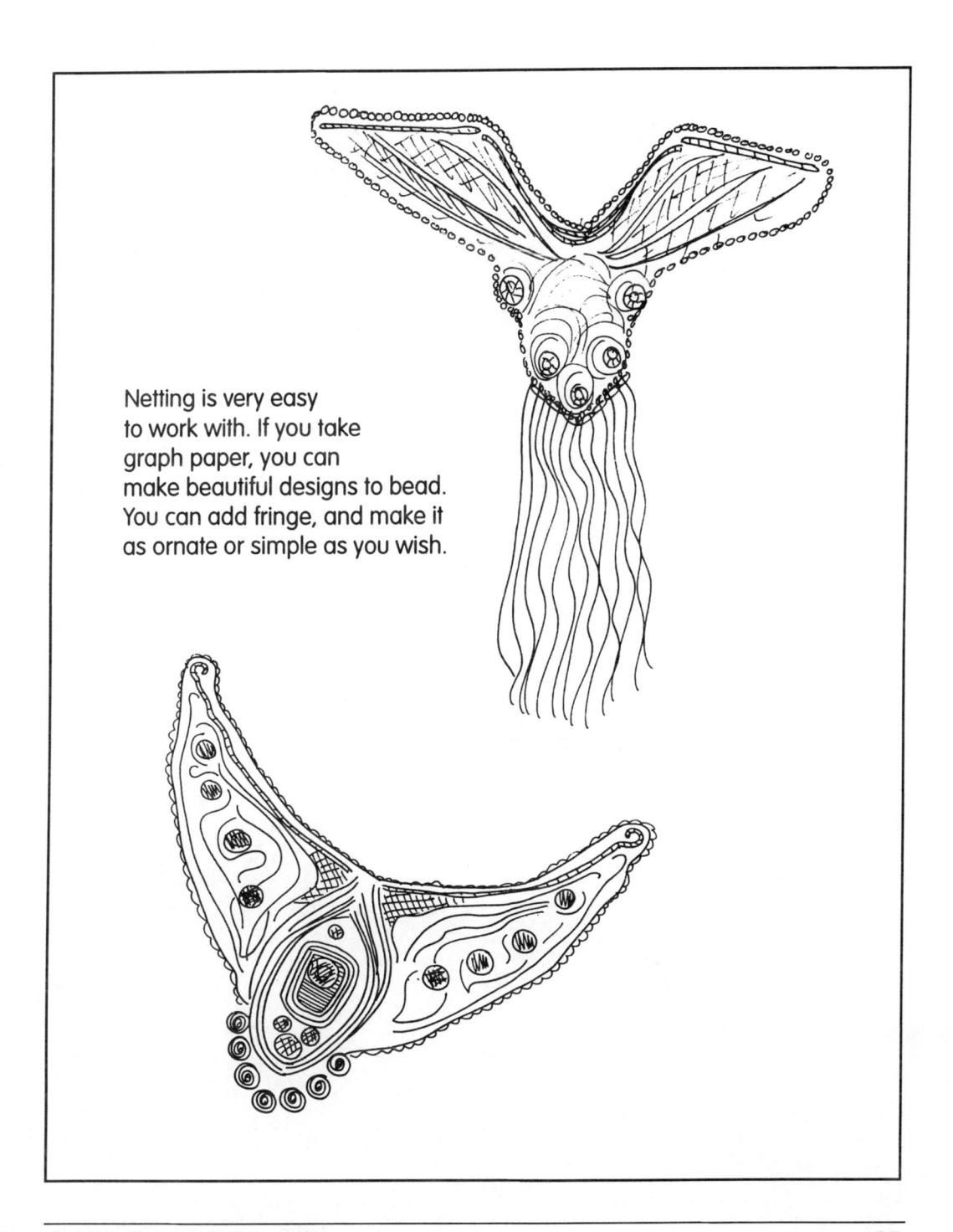

Netting is very easy to work with. If you take graph paper, you can make beautiful designs to bead. You can add fringe, and make it as ornate or simple as you wish.

The Beading on Fabric Book 35

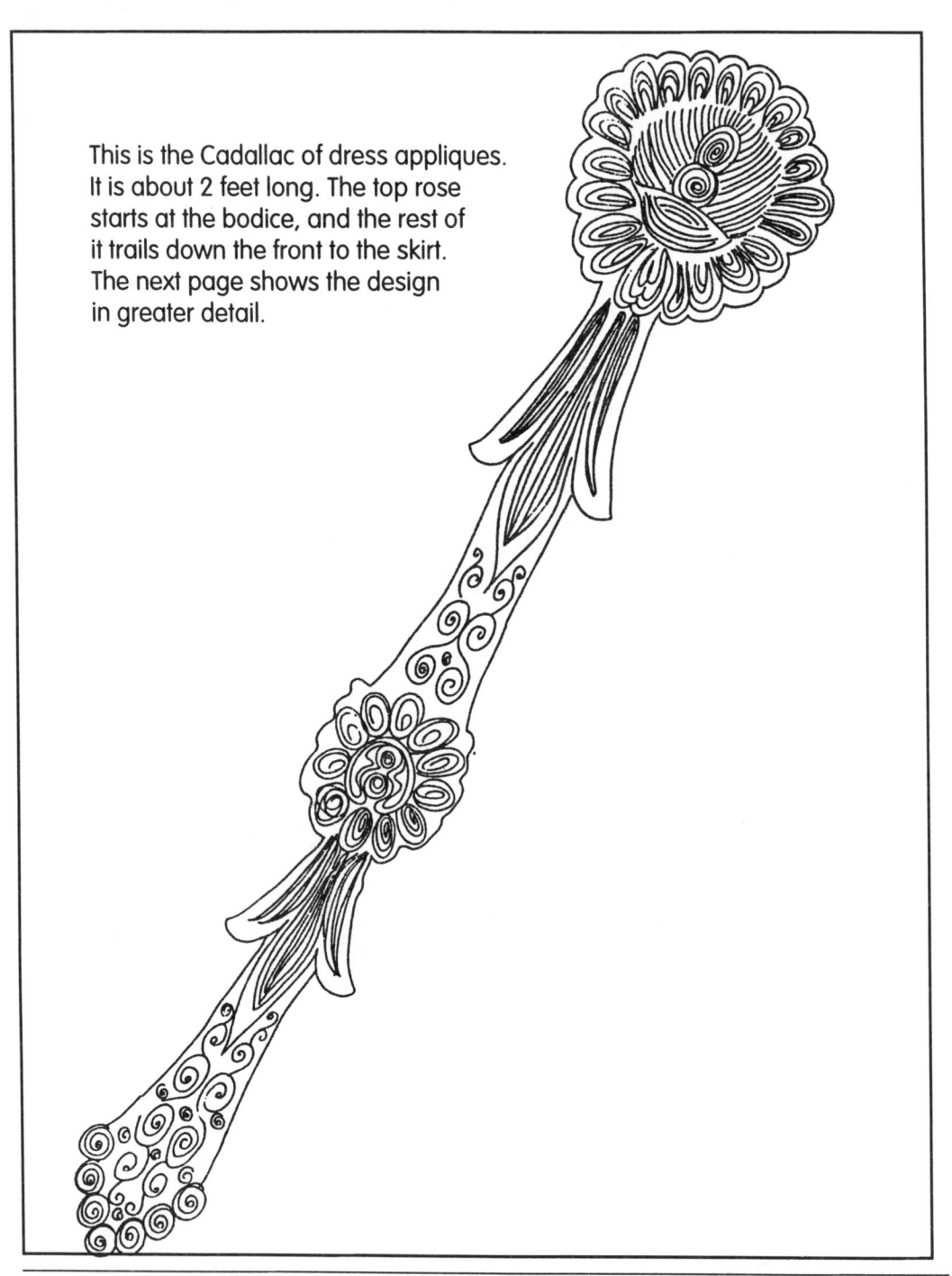

This is the Cadallac of dress appliques. It is about 2 feet long. The top rose starts at the bodice, and the rest of it trails down the front to the skirt. The next page shows the design in greater detail.

The Beading on Fabric Book

The Beading on Fabric Book 37

Beaded Purses

These beaded purses have never gone out of style. Worked on satin fabric, they dress up any outfit. You can also bead shoes to match.

MATERIALS
- Satin fabric (see pattern on next page for size)
- Bronze bugle beads (one hank)
- Peach colored 3mm Czech faceted crystal
- One foot bronze metallic cord (for strap)
- Beige nymo in "B" weight
- English beading needle size #12
- One sewing machine

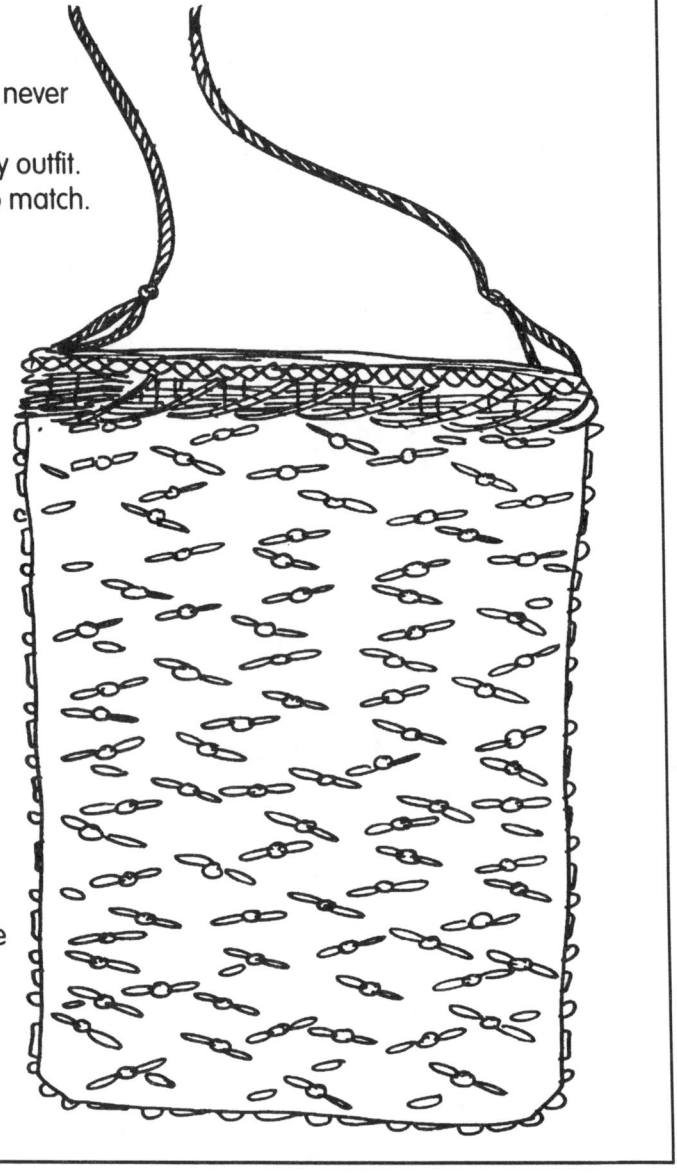

4 1/2"

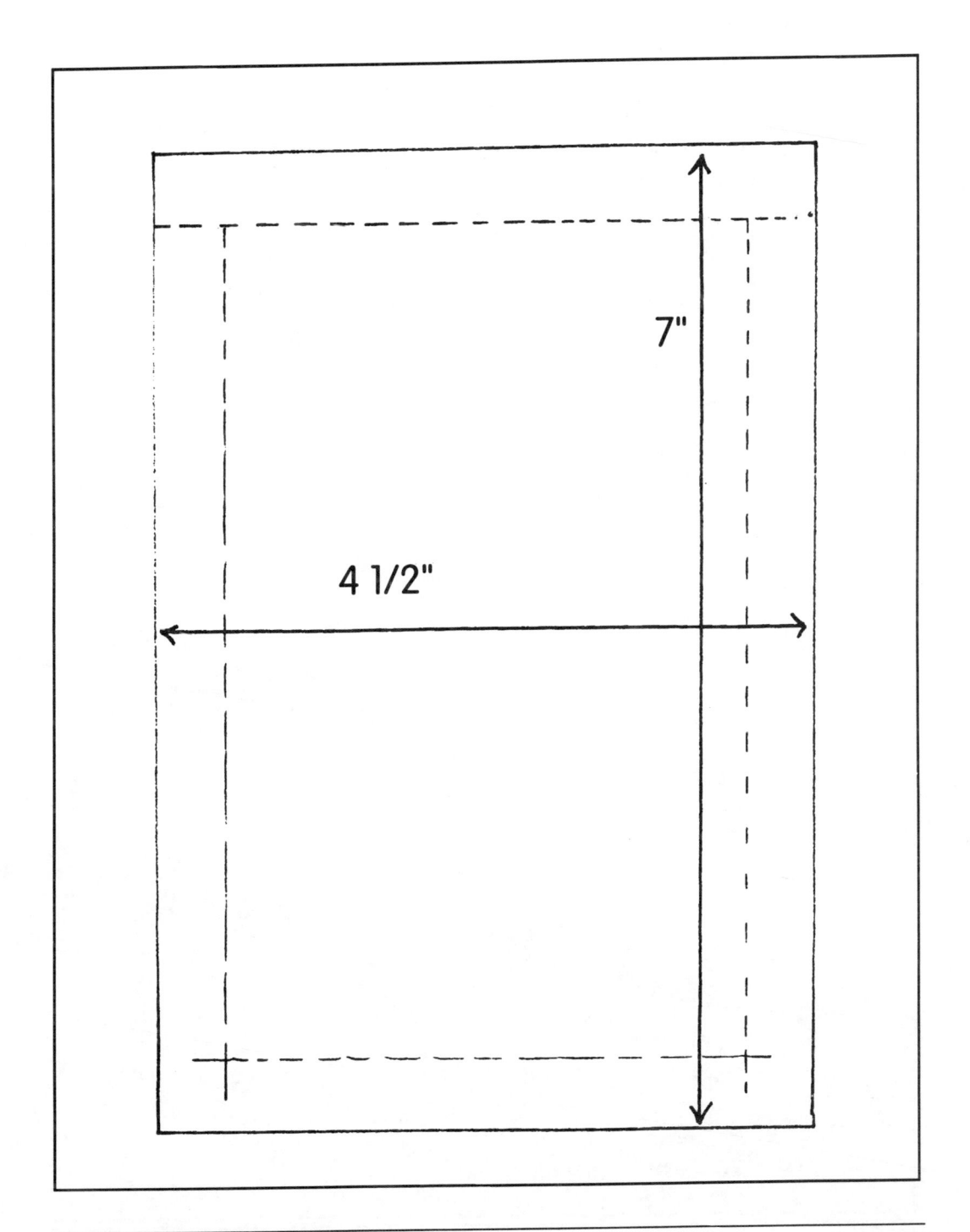

7"

The Beading on Fabric Book

Cut two pieces of satin fabric. With wrong sides of fabric together, machine sew seams along the 2 sides and bottom. Turn rightside out, and fold in the top edge. Carefully press.

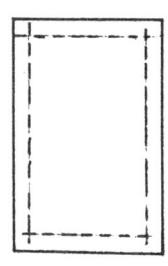

Working in the Running Stitch, alternate bugle beads and crystal around the side and bottom seams.

Bead the top of the purse with one row of bugles, one row of crystals, then 5 rows of bugles.

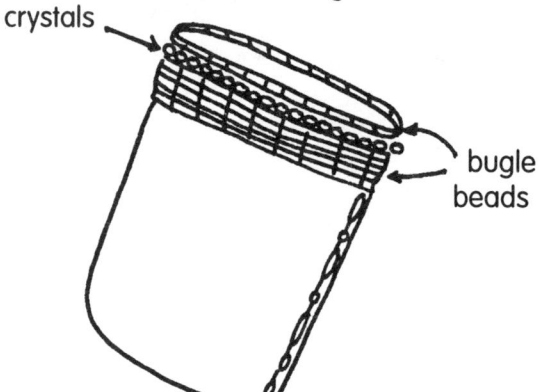

crystals

bugle beads

With 4 bugle beads, "wrap" the five rows of bugles.

Bead a crisscross pattern with units of one bugle, one crystal, one bugle.

Cut the strap to length, and attach.

The Beading on Fabric Book

Beaded Purse #2

Pearls always add something to the designs you use them in. This beaded purse was inspired by the sixties, when this type of beading was very popular. The loops of beads give a lot of movement, and the teal satin sets off the warmth of the creamy pearls.

MATERIALS

- Satin fabric (see pattern on next page for size)
- Forty-five 10mm pearls (if you plan to bead both sides, you'll need eighty-seven)
- Seventeen 6mm pearls (23 for both sides)
- 122 7x5mm AB Czech crystal (206 for both sides)
- Two cut seedbeads (one hank)
- Nymo in "B" weight
- #12 English beading needle
- One sewing machine
- Jeweler's

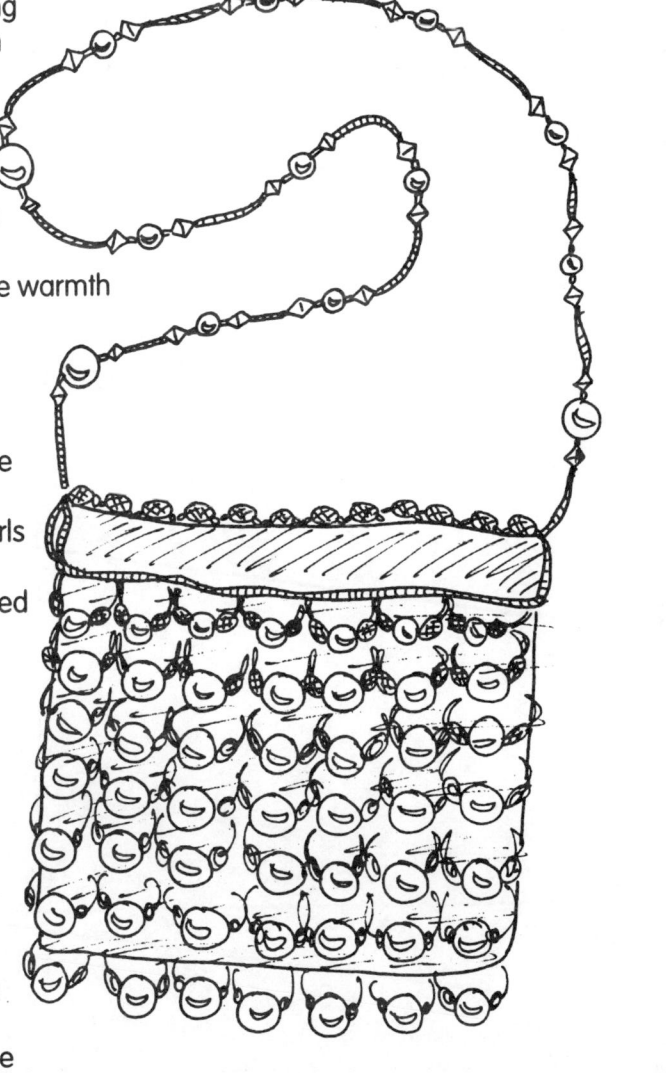

The Beading on Fabric Book

6"

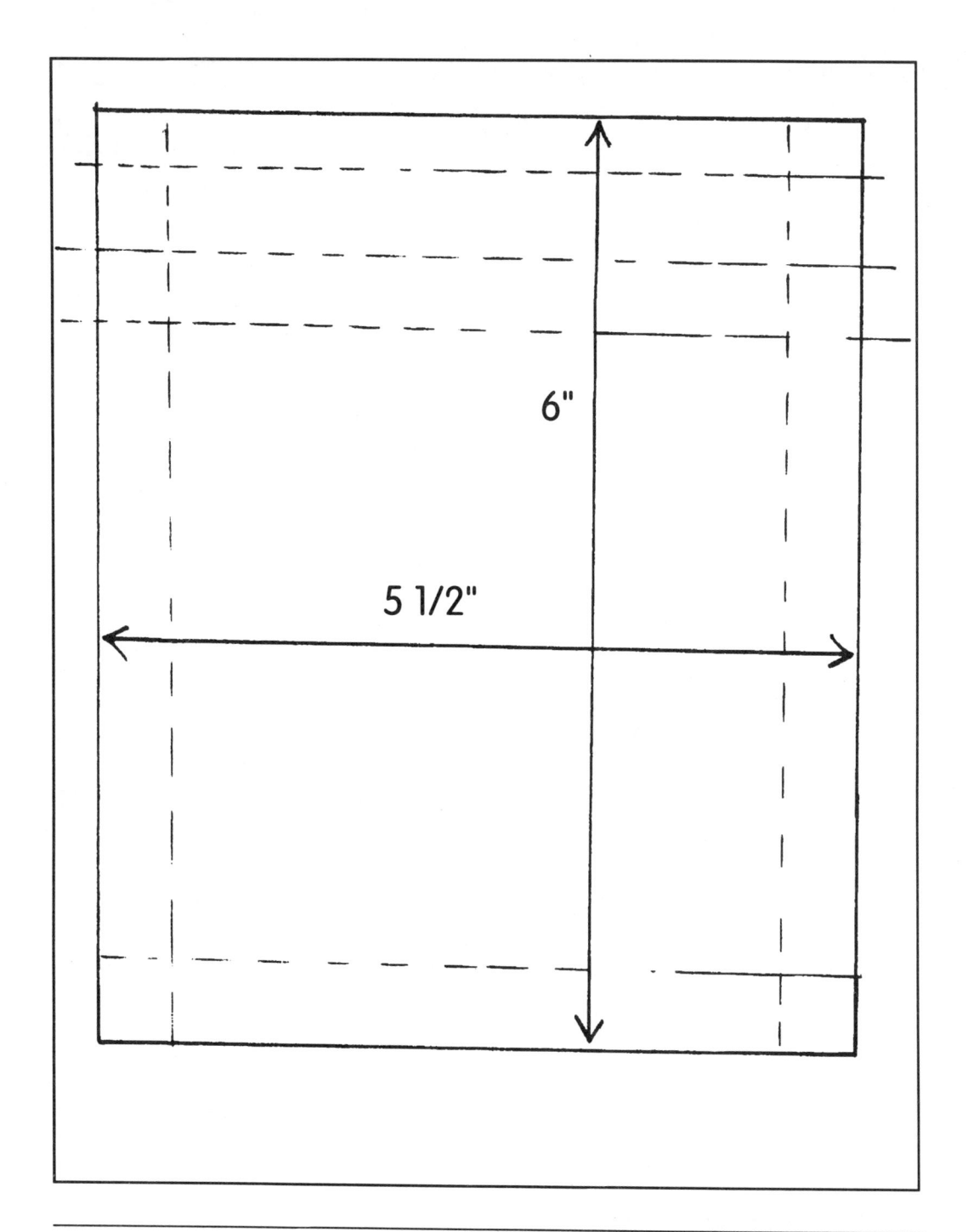

5 1/2"

Cut your fabric and sew the seams on the sewing machine. Fold the top of the purse to make a one-inch cuff. Handsew your inside seam, and press carefully.

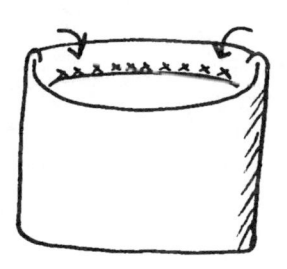

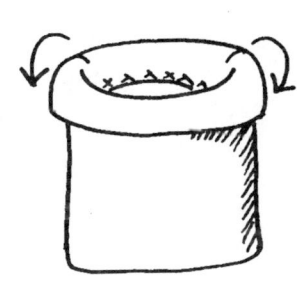

Using the Three-Bead Method, bead the edge around the cuff with seedbeads.

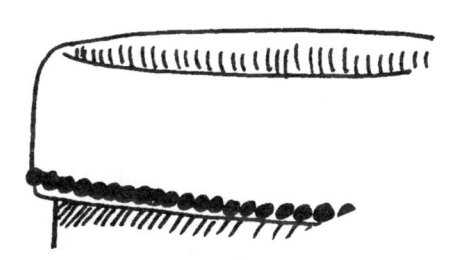

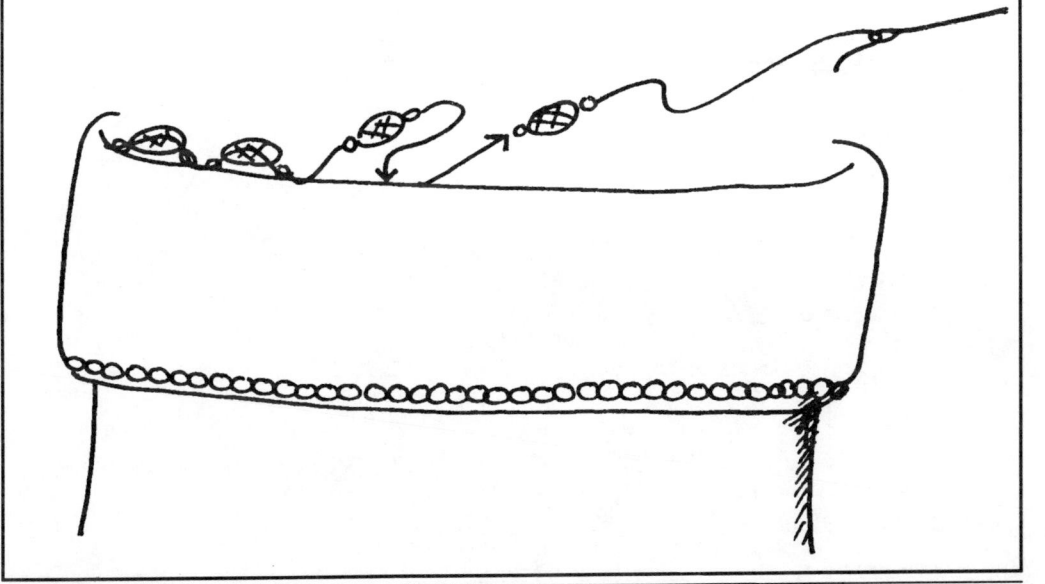

The Beading on Fabric Book

Starting on your bottom edge, stitch your loops, using the larger pearls. There are 7 loops across. The loops are 3 seedbeads, one crystal, one pearl, one crystal, 3 seedbeads.

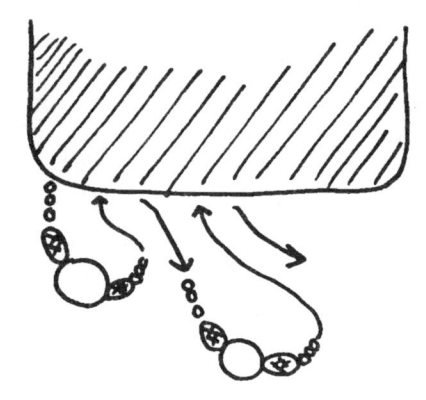

Work your way up, using the smaller pearls for the top row. This will look more even if you very lightly measure and mark your rows.

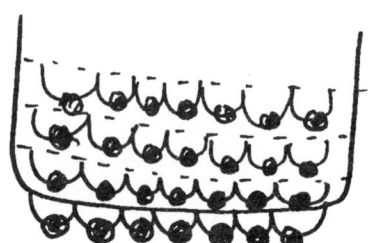

Bead two decorative rows of seedbeads on the sides near the strap,

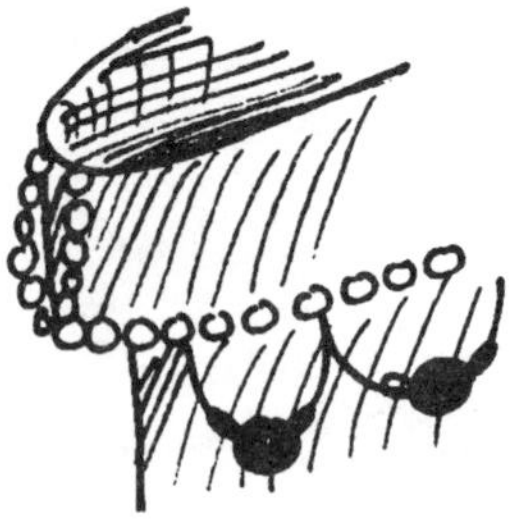

Bead your strap. The pattern is ten seedbeads, *one crystal, one seedbead, one pearl, one seedbead, one crystal, five seedbeads. Repeat from *, and end with ten seedbeads. Use your 3 larger pearls at the ends and middle of the strap as accents. Secure your ends and cement your knots.

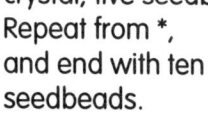

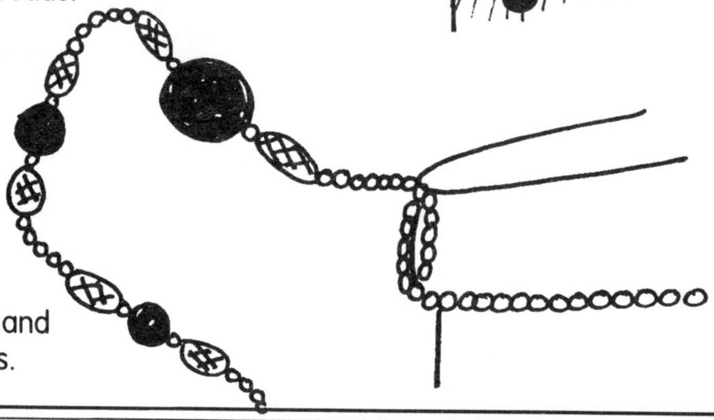

The Beading on Fabric Book

Beaded Medallion

This embellishment can go anywhere. If you use black cabochons in unusual shapes (squares, rectangles, teardrops, etc.) it adds a beautiful drama to the piece. The peacock-colored seedbeads are very popular, and this can be worn as an embellishment on a hat, dress, purse, or made into a brooch. It was worked on a scrap piece of linen, and there is a nice substance and solidness to the piece.

MATERIALS
- Small piece of linen fabric
- A mixture of teardrop, round, and square cabochons
- One hank each of bronze, peacock, and indigo seedbeads
- #12 English beading needle
- "B" weight nymo thread
- Embroidery hoop
- Cement
- (Optional) pin back

The Beading on Fabric Book

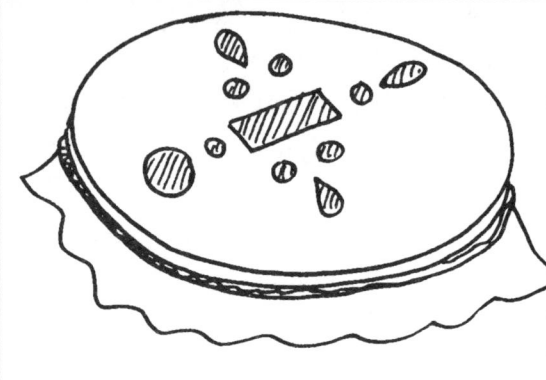

Cement your cabochons to your fabric.

Using your bronze seedbeads, outline each cabochon with the Three-Bead Method. Then, make a second row with the indigo seedbeads.

Working evenly, add rows of seedbeads to each cabochon until they start to meet.

Fill in with seedbeads to complete your circle pattern.

To make a brooch, back with a piece of leather the same size as the circle of beads. Fold the ends inside carefully trim the edges, and whipstitch. You can add beads to your whipstitch. There are other patterns for this in The Best Little Beading Book, another book in our series of beading books.

46

The Beading on Fabric Book

Kuba-Inspired Picture Frame

Inspired by the beaded Kuba collars from Africa, this project can be made into a picture frame or a mirror. It is very alive with color, and lights up a room.

Part of the charm is the use of cowrie shells and African trade beads. The patterned seedbeads add a boldness, and the mix of color and texture have a beautiful energy.

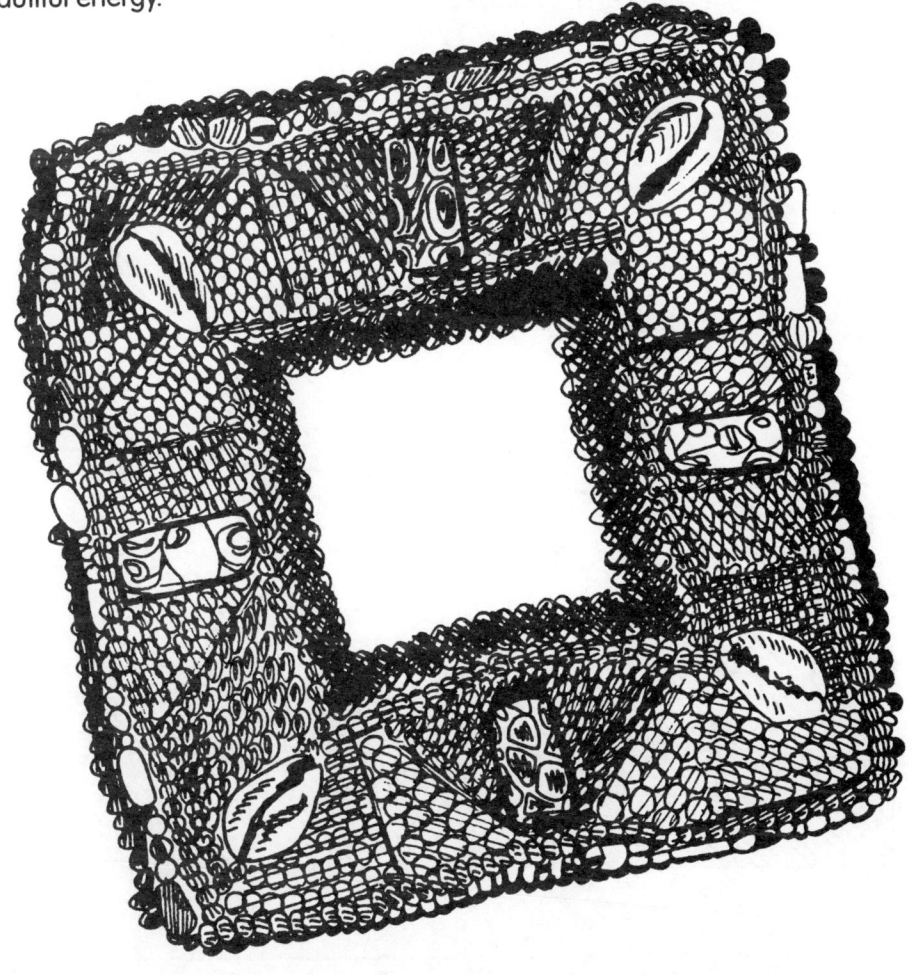

The Beading on Fabric Book

MATERIALS
- One piece of Aida cloth, 12"x 12"
- Four African trade beads
- Four cowrie shells
- Seedbeads ranging from 9/0 to 7/0 in the following colors:
    black, red, light blue, brown, white, gold striped, medium blue, red, white and blue striped, black and yellow striped
    (the richness of texture comes from the mixing of sizes of beads)
- One strand of African Christmas beads
- Cardboard for backing and framework
- #10 English beading needles
- "B" weight nymo
- Cement   - Piece of cotton batting, 5" x 5"

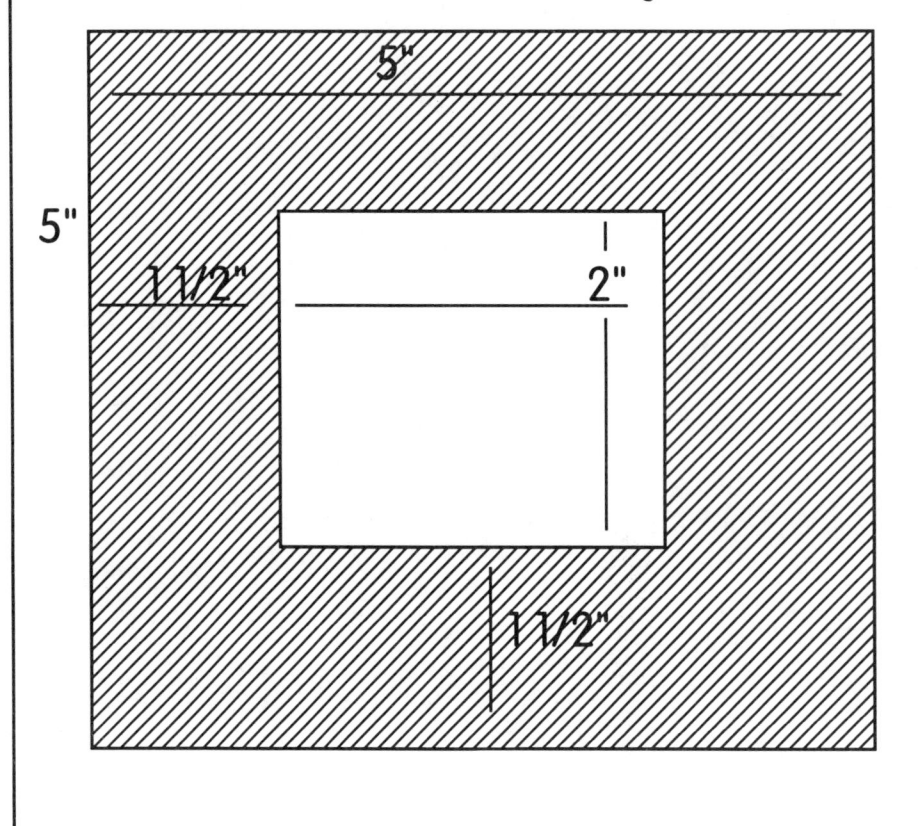

The Beading on Fabric Book

The first thing you want to do is sew the cowrie shells and trade beads into position. This helps you keep things symmetrical as you bead.

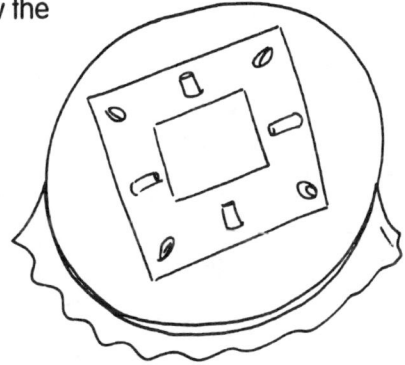

The trade beads are attached like any other bead (thru the hole). Cowrie shells are tricker, because they're not drilled. Position them on your cloth, and bring your thread up from the wrong side of the fabric. Loop it over the shell, and let it fall into the groove. Pull tightly, and bring your needle back into the fabric on the other side. You shouldhave caught the shell in the loop, and adjust the tension so it is snug. Repeat this a couple of times , so it's strong and can't break the thread.

The color pattern is:

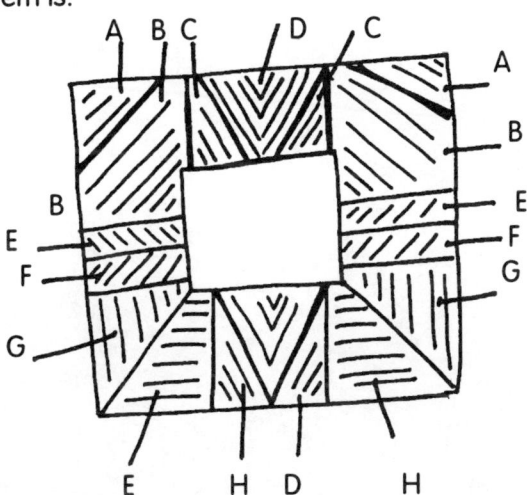

A: brown, B: white, C: light blue, D: black, E: red, F: gold striped, G: red/white/blue

The Beading on Fabric Book

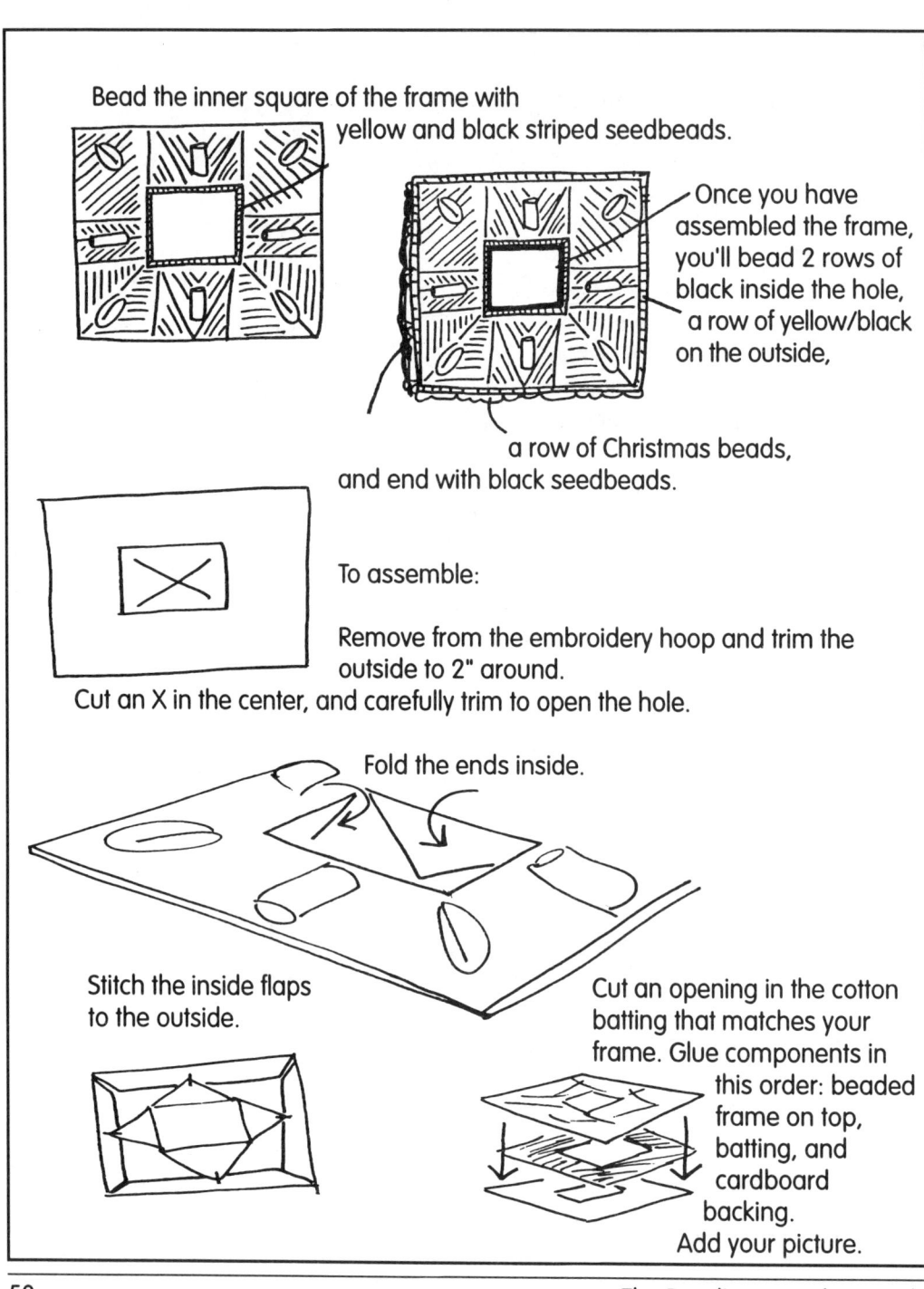

Bead the inner square of the frame with yellow and black striped seedbeads.

Once you have assembled the frame, you'll bead 2 rows of black inside the hole, a row of yellow/black on the outside, a row of Christmas beads, and end with black seedbeads.

To assemble:

Remove from the embroidery hoop and trim the outside to 2" around.
Cut an X in the center, and carefully trim to open the hole.

Fold the ends inside.

Stitch the inside flaps to the outside.

Cut an opening in the cotton batting that matches your frame. Glue components in this order: beaded frame on top, batting, and cardboard backing.
Add your picture.

The Beading on Fabric Book

About the Author

Wendy Simpson Conner is no stranger to beads. As a third-generation bead artist, she grew up with beads from a very early age. Her grandmother was the jewelry and costume designer for the Ziegfeld Follies.

Being from a creative family, Wendy spent her childhood doing many types of crafts in a rural community. ("There just wasn't anything else to do!"). Over the years, she has mastered many techniques, but beads have remained her first love.

She worked as a designer in television for awhile, and also has a strong illustration background (she always insists on doing her own illustrations).

Wendy has been teaching vocational beadwork classes for San Diego Community Colleges and the Grossmont Adult School District for many years. She not only teaches beading technique, but also the dynamics of running your own jewelry business.

Her first book, The Best Little Beading Book, was the result of many of her classroom handouts. All of her books, including The Beaded Lampshade Book, The Magical Beaded Medicine Bag Book, The "Knotty" Macrame and Beading Book, The Beaded Watchband Book, The Chain & Crystal Book, The Beaded Jewelry for a Wedding Book, The Children's Beading Book, The Cat Lover's Beaded Project Book, and The Wire Bending Book, have been very popular. They are part of **The Beading Books Series,** a collection of 25 books devoted to preserving beading techniques and history. Many of these books are also available in kit form. These kits include the original book, plus materials for making the projects shown.

Wendy designs jewelry for several television shows, as well as the celebrities on them.

Recently, she produced, wrote and directed The Bead Movement, the critically acclaimed one hour documentary which examines the world's fascination with beads. This is now also available in a 27 minute director's cut.

Wendy is available to teach workshops. If you are interested, please contact her through the Interstellar Publishing Company, Post Office Box 2215, La Mesa, California, 91943.

If you have any beading questions, you may email them to Interstlr@aol.com. Wendy also writes the Ask Aunt Beady feature in our website, www.interstellarpublishing.com.

The Beading on Fabric Book

Interstellar
TRADING & PUBLISHING COMPANY

Other Books, Kits, and Videos By the Interstellar Trading & Publishing Company:

The Best Little Beading Book
The Beaded Lampshade Book
The Magical Beaded Medicine Bag Book
The "Knotty" Macrame & Beading Book
The Beaded Watchband Book
The Chain & Crystal Book
The Beaded Jewelry for a Wedding Book
The Children's Beading Book
The Cat Lover's Beaded Project Book
The Wire Bending Book
The Beading On Fabric Book
The "Knotty" Macrame Kit
The Beaded Watchband Kit
The Magical Beaded Medicine Bag Kit
The Children's Beading Kit
"The Bead Movement", a one hour documentary about beads
"The Bead Movement/Director's Cut" (27 min.)

If you would like a catalog of other titles and forthcoming books from the Interstellar Trading & Publishing Company, please send a stamped, self-addressed envelope to:

**THE INTERSTELLAR TRADING & PUBLISHING COMPANY
POST OFFICE BOX 2215 •LA MESA, CALIFORNIA, 91943**

visit our website at www.interstellarpublishing.com